"*Listening to Cougar* indeed! And hearing some of our finest writers, the echoes of of pure joy that say so much about who become."

—**BILL McKIBBEN**, AUTHOR OF *The Bill McKibben Reader*

"[An] illuminating new collection . . . there are at least five or six essays that contribute greatly to the growing literature on mountain lion behavior and conservation."

—**TIM HULL**, *Tucson Weekly*

"[T]he stories all promote peaceful co-existence by appealing to human tolerance and understanding of what this animal's absence would mean to the ecosystem and to the human soul."

—**SANDY NELSON**, *Santa Fe New Mexican*

"As long as there are still cougars out there, wilderness itself survives. By gathering the best stories to be found from people who have personally experienced the great cat, Marc Bekoff and Cara Blessley Lowe have brought our most elusive animal to life."

—**DAVID ROTHENBERG**, AUTHOR OF *Why Birds Sing* AND *Thousand Mile Song*

"Elegant and powerful, cougars are icons of wilderness that stir our dreams and emotions. The vibrant tales of encounters with cougars in this anthology express not only admiration for this adaptable predator but also convey that its survival is our moral obligation. The book is a timely and thoughtful blend of natural history and evocation of a mysterious creature."

—**GEORGE B. SCHALLER**, WILDLIFE CONSERVATION SOCIETY

"From carnivore expert [Marc] Bekoff to nature writers Rick Bass and Barry Lopez and to poet Gary Gildner, each short contribution leaves the reader with a respect for the animal that contrasts with the coldness of the human attack statistics at the back of the book."

—*Conservation Magazine*

"*Listening to Cougar* captures the grace, beauty, and majesty of cougars, and powerfully conveys what cougars mean to people through their own experiences and stories. A must-read for the public, ranchers, scientists, managers, and conservationists, this well-written collectiongives voice to views that until now have gone little-heeded by policymakers, and will help cougars by helping us find common ground."

—SUSAN G. CLARK, PROFESSOR OF WILDLIFE ECOLOGY AND POLICY SCIENCES, YALE UNIVERSITY

"This spellbinding tribute to the *Puma concolor* honors the big cat's presence on the land and in our psyches."

—YUBANET.COM

"I especially enjoyed the return to old school naturalist writings, celebrating writers who truly know their subject and write about it as scientists and storytellers, from the head and from the heart."

—KATHY BROWN, PARK RANGER / DISTRICT NATURALIST, ROCKY MOUNTAIN NATIONAL PARK

"A far-ranging, inspired collection of voices speaking for cougars and seeing the world through the eyes of this great but vulnerable cat."

—BRENDA PETERSON, AUTHOR OF *Build Me an Ark: A Life with Animals*

"In *Listening To Cougar,* reverence for cougar lives on through the power of story from those who have been lucky enough to catch a glimpse of the shadow cat in the wild. This collection of essays brings to life the power and majesty of this large cat and whether or not you have been fortunate enough to see one in the wild, these gripping stories bring home the importance that these animals remain living wild and free in our natural world."

—SHARON NEGRI, EXECUTIVE DIRECTOR AND FOUNDER, WILDFUTURES, A PROJECT OF EARTH ISLAND INSTITUTE

LISTENING
to COUGAR

LISTENING
to COUGAR

Marc Bekoff and
Cara Blessley Lowe, Editors

UNIVERSITY PRESS OF COLORADO

Published by the University Press of Colorado
5589 Arapahoe Avenue, Suite 206C
Boulder, Colorado 80303

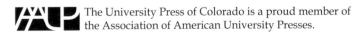 The University Press of Colorado is a proud member of
the Association of American University Presses.

The University Press of Colorado is a cooperative publishing enterprise
supported, in part, by Adams State College, Colorado State University,
Fort Lewis College, Mesa State College, Metropolitan State College of
Denver, University of Colorado, University of Northern Colorado, and
Western State College of Colorado.

∞ The paper used in this publication meets the minimum requirements
of the American National Standard for Information Sciences — Perma-
nence of Paper for Printed Library Materials. ANSI Z39.48-1992

Library of Congress Cataloging-in-Publication Data

Listening to cougar / Marc Bekoff and Cara Blessley Lowe, editors.
    p. cm.
  Includes bibliographical references.
  ISBN 978-0-87081-894-3 (hardcover : alk. paper)
  ISBN 978-0-87081-936-0 (pbk. : alk. paper) 1. Puma — Anecdotes. I.
Bekoff, Marc. II. Lowe, Cara Blessley.
  QL737.C23L57 2007
  599.75'24 — dc22

                                                              2007033012

Design by Daniel Pratt

17 16 15 14 13 12 11   10 9 8 7 6 5 4 3 2

This book is dedicated to Wildlife Biologist Rocky Spencer, who spent his life educating people how to peacefully co-exist with wildlife. In his final years, he worked extensively with cougars. He loved this work immensely and learned a great deal about listening to cougar.

For all wild animals — may you remain wild at heart.

MB

For Jen, ever courageous.

CBL

CONTENTS

CONTENTS

Contents

CONTENTS

FOREWORD

When I was about nine years old, I found, in the secondhand bookstore that I haunted as a child, a book about a wonderful friendship between a boy and a wild cougar. I cannot remember the plot, and although I have searched and searched among the hundreds of books that fill every room of our house, I cannot find that little paperback with its orange/red cover. But it gave me a fascination for cougars—also known as mountain lions or pumas. I wanted to find out more about the beautiful big cat of the Americas, with its dark rounded ears, white muzzle, and glorious sand-colored coat. The cat that would never hurt you, I was sure, unless provoked.

I have still never seen a wild cougar—most people haven't. But when a female made her den in a cave in the mountains just opposite the National Museum of Wildlife Art in Jackson Hole, a rare opportunity for watching cougars arose. Tom Mangelsen, wildlife photographer extraordinaire, spent days with his long lens trained on that den. He and scores of visitors observed the three kittens as they emerged into the daylight on uncertain legs, and noted how, over the next couple of weeks, they grew stronger and increasingly playful. And then, one morning, they had gone. Led by their mother into the dangers of a world that is, by and large, hostile to cougars.

It was Tom who introduced me to the horrible situation of the cougar in North America. First he showed me the photos and video he had taken of that female—whom we named Spirit—and her adorable kittens. Playing with mother's tail. Playing with a feather. No wonder so many people spent so long watching that den, waiting for the rare glimpses of mother and young. And then, after we had spent a wonderful day in Yellowstone, he showed me the video footage taken by Cara of an outfitter making the decision to "harvest" the "young male" who is crouched as high in the tree as he can while the hunting dogs bay and lunge at its base. Such a beautiful animal—and, as it transpired, a female. One moment vivid with life, the next a dead body. Her beingness evaporated into the cold winter air. I was shocked and sickened.

What an ending to an otherwise perfect day in Yellowstone. I had seen wild bears for the first time: a very big male grizzly and a female black bear with cubs. And feasted my eyes on that glorious landscape, watched the sunset over the mountains. And then, suddenly, that video footage of sudden violent death. That was when Tom told me about The Cougar Fund, which he had started. I offered to sit on the board and gradually learned more and more about the persecution of the Americas' big cat. Horrible facts. Until that day, I did not know that it was legal in many states to hunt cougars with dogs. I had no idea that in some states they are classified as "vermin." In Texas, for example, cougars of any age can be killed in any way at any time of year, with guns, bows and arrows, and from cars. They can be trapped and poisoned—even tiny kittens. I didn't know that in many states it costs only $30, and sometimes less, to buy a license to kill a cougar; that annual quotas can be suddenly increased (in one instance from two to twenty) by Fish and Wildlife authorities, even when there has been no sound research behind such a decision.

And even when there are regulations, they can be difficult to enforce. Tom explained that in Wyoming it is illegal to kill a female with cubs at her side, or cubs younger than one year, even during the six-month hunting season. But there is a 75 percent chance that a female will have cubs during the hunting season, and cubs will rarely travel with their mother, especially if they are less than four months old. If their mother is shot, her kittens may die and, as a result, the hunter has, perhaps unknowingly, violated the law. As we have seen, even an outfitter who should have known better couldn't tell the difference between a male and a female cougar.

Only in California is there a ban on hunting mountain lions, thanks initially to the efforts of Margaret Owings. I knew her well, and she asked me to write a letter in support of mountain lion protection — which I was, of course, delighted to do. But although her efforts were successful, a property owner only needs to complain that a mountain lion has become a "nuisance" and he or she is usually able to get permission to kill it. And such complaints become ever more common as more and more people crowd into California, many of them anxious to avoid the fumes and bustle of city life, seeking to establish a closer connection to nature, seeking permission to build their houses ever deeper into the last remaining wildlife habitats. No wonder encounters with cougars are becoming ever more frequent as human beings invade their land. And only too often the human interlopers seek not to establish a connection with a cougar who lives nearby, where he has always lived, but to dispose of it for fear that the animal might harm them or their children or their pets. All too often, the cougar will be shot.

Yet across America there have been very few recorded instances of cougar attacks on humans. Prior to 1992, there were only ten. And even though the number of conflicts has risen in recent years (seven between 1992 and 2002) as people move further into cougar country, domestic dogs are still responsible for many more attacks. (People driving cars kill hundreds more people than do cougars—or any wild animal!) It has always seemed to me that if we choose to move into the territory of cougars—or bears or any other wild animals—we should learn to live with them and be prepared, like Marc and many of the people featured in this book, to come to terms with the possibility of meeting a cougar on a hike. Learn how to behave, carry a can of bear spray in case of an emergency. And keep in mind that there is less chance of a cougar (or bear or bison or any other large wild animal) attacking us in the wilderness than there is of being run down by a car, or mugged in a city.

Some people understand. Last year I visited Charlie Knowles in his house, which is surrounded by wilderness. He told me how he had come down early one morning and seen his cat staring fixedly through the glass in the living room into the backyard. She was almost touching the glass with her nose. He kept still and followed her gaze. And there, sitting just outside the door and gazing with equal fascination, it seemed, at the cat, was a magnificent young mountain lion. For a moment the tableau held, and then the cougar, sensing his presence perhaps, turned and vanished into the dawn. Charlie would never dream of harming his wild neighbors.

Soon after I became involved with The Cougar Fund, we convened an exciting gathering of cougar people from various organizations and different parts of the country to discuss ways of collaboration that would benefit mountain lions as well as all our organizations. It was good to see so much passion and meet some of the people who are working so hard to protect the big cats. The Cougar Fund works in cooperation with the Jane Goodall Institute's environmental and humanitarian youth program, Roots & Shoots. In this way we are helping spread educational material to our members and teaching young people about cougars and their behavior and the desperate need to help them. I hope that this book, with its sometimes tragic, sometimes moving accounts of people and cougars, will go a long way to helping people understand what is really going on and how desperately the cougars, and those championing them, need all our help today.

I am writing this introduction on New Year's Eve, 2006. On the wall opposite me is one of my favorite photos, taken by Tom, of Spirit and her three kittens. A devoted mother struggling to raise her young in a dangerous world. And all the wide-eyed expectations of the young ones, playful and quite unprepared for the harsh, human-dominated world into which their mother must, perforce, lead them. I wonder, as Tom and Cara and I have so often wondered, if any of those four vital cougar beings are still living. I picked up the phone and dialed Tom's number. And what an extraordinary coincidence. He is, as I write, sitting in his car with his camera lens trained onto a pair of ears. A female cougar with the silhouette of Jackson Hole buildings behind her in the darkening evening sky. The small group of people watching is keeping quiet about her presence—she is too close to town. In spite of some progress with the officials, we all still fear that the Wyoming Game and Fish will decide to have her shot, seeing her as a potential danger. In fact she is peacefully waiting for darkness to fall and then, Tom thinks, she will move silently back into the safer mountains.

New Year's Eve is a time for memories, and I am in my room in the house in England where I grew up. Many of the books I read as a child are on the shelves—although not the one about the boy and the wild cougar. In my lifetime the world has changed so much. That lost book was written in a time when there were fewer people on the planet, more areas of wilderness, more hopeful opportunities for such jungle friendships. In the imagination of a child, anything is possible. Where adults so often see fear, children see the potential of adventure, as the boy did with the wild cougar. Perhaps by bridging these two worlds we can come to terms with how to coexist with this animal, for the cougar's survival ultimately depends on our tolerance of it living among us.

Thankfully, there are still some wild places left. A few years ago, as I sat with a small group of young people, sharing stories around a log fire, a young man told me about a journey he had made in a small boat in an utterly remote part of Central America. One afternoon his guide left the main river and turned up a small tributary that flowed through dense forest. And suddenly there was a puma, crouched on the trunk of a tree that had fallen across the water, drinking. As the boat appeared, he raised his head and, quite calmly, looked at them, with the rays of the sun shining through the canopy and glinting on the drops of water that dripped from his chin. Then he stood and moved away, unafraid, into whatever the evening held for him.

—JANE GOODALL PH.D., DBE
FOUNDER OF THE JANE GOODALL INSTITUTE AND
UN MESSENGER OF PEACE
www.janegoodall.org

ACKNOWLEDGMENTS

In 2005, we were looking for another way to tell the story of an animal whose life is increasingly under siege. The wonderful anthology *Shadow Cat* served as an early inspiration for this collection. It was within that book's pages that my initial interest in and research about cougars began. It is amazing what a single book can spark. Marc Bekoff, with decades of field study under his belt, has authored and edited many such volumes, and it was only natural that I turn to him to guide this relative newcomer through the drill of submission requests and acceptances, contracts and sheer knowledge. Thank you, Marc.

Darrin Pratt, our editor at the University Press of Colorado, embraced the idea from the beginning. We are blessed and lucky to have the gift of such enthusiasm and experience to bring *Listening to Cougar* to life. Tom Mangelsen, the dearest of friends, is ever generous in extending the permissions to use his photograph for our cover. All of Tom's pictures are taken in the wild, and even though he waited more than fifty years to see a cougar, I can honestly say that his patience paid off. No photographer has a better, more sensitive collection of wild cougar images — or of any wildlife — than Tom. They are a rare commodity in today's photographic market that is bloated with pictures of captive animals.

This book would not exist without the gifted voices of our contributors. The most gracious of thanks to you who have endured the time and effort required to create *Listening to Cougar*. It was important to us that the range of voices include all stakeholders, and although state game agency officials may not have been in the position to officially submit their writings, we appreciate your candid conversations, your time, and the fine work you are doing on behalf of this magnificent creature.

A million heartfelt thanks to Lyn Dalebout, who, in her poetic and intuitive way, suggested a title that stuck. To Sue Cedarholm, who has helped me in so many ways during this, and other, projects. To Jane Goodall, a friend from the start and ever a source of strength. To Sara Carlson, and her exemplary attention to detail. To Ted Kerasote, for making the time to put his experience on paper. To Susan G. Clark, and all the advice over the years. To Jim McNutt, who suggested the J. Frank Dobie piece. To Ken Logan and Linda Sweanor, my first mentors — thank you for being there for an endless stream of questions over the years and for guiding us through your Cuyamaca study area so many years ago. To my Antelope Flats neighbors, John Craighead and the late Frank Craighead, who carried the torch for so many years. To Maurice Hornocker, whose work remains an inspiration. To Wayne Suda, who had the courage to include me on a cougar hunting expedition, and the presence to attend the film premiere. Thank you for sharing your side of the story. To Rick Hopkins, who is always available at the drop of a hat, and who possesses a lifetime of knowledge of *Puma concolor*, without whom we'd be lost. To Corey Rutledge, "cat herder" extraordinaire. To the Buffetts: Howard, Devon, Howie, and the late Susie, for joining us for breakfast that fortuitous morning in Moose and for standing by this species. To Bob Smith, organizational wonder. To Shawn Meisl; because of you I can sleep at night.

To Sharon Negri, who leads by example, and embodies the quiet strength and power of cougar in all her work.

Thanks also to our friends and families. To my parents, Beatrice Rose and Oscar Bekoff, for their incredible and unwavering support over the years. To Leslie and Gregg Goodyear, Thiele Robinson, Michelle Jungquist, Andrea Baxter, Cami Runnalls, Elena Luaces Dryer, Sherrie Watterson, Anna Garcia-Graña, Deb O'Neill, Kim Eilian, Rick Smolan, Kia Jam, Steven and Adrian Goff, Chris Papouchis, Joe Pytka, Jack and Dana Turner, Bert and Meg Raynes, Brooke Williams and Terry Tempest Williams, Lee and Ed Riddell, Chuck Schneeback, Derek and Sophie Craighead, Al and Jean Lowe, Charlie Craighead, Shirley Craighead, Chuck and Barbara Herz, Lyle and Amy McReynolds, Rob and Tricia Morphew, Ned and Amanda Pinkerton—fortresses of friendship. To my parents, Webb and Donna Blessley, steadfast in every way. Without the behind-the-scenes support of *my* first assistant director, Sonny Lowe, this book would have taken substantially more hours, days, and months—thank you.

To all of you who care so much about this animal, and to you who work so hard to champion its place in our world. No matter our perspectives, may we continue to work together to see that this species survives its challenges.

Always, to Spirit. A messenger of the wild, thank you for what you've given us—may we do your kind justice.

LISTENING to COUGAR

INTRODUCING COUGAR

We are sorry to hear that Mr. Fred Cole is no better. Miss Ruth Johnson has been in for the past week with an ingrowing toenail. Mr. J. G. Johnson, merchant, is worrying considerable about his hogs eating so much corn and not fattening.

Messrs. Winfield Powers and Cleveland Gordon were calling on their lady friends last Sunday night in Loudoun, and on their way home were chased by a panther.

—SANDY HOOK NEWS, OCTOBER 19, 1906

Winfield Powers was my maternal great-great-grandfather and Sandy Hook is the small hamlet where my mother's family hails from. Today, the town is nothing more than a few ramshackle houses along the Potomac River in western Maryland, at the point where the Potomac converges with the Shenandoah River. Dense woods engulf the land, and to this day it remains surprisingly wild. Two hundred fifty miles away and three hundred years earlier in what is now Manhattan, a vast commercial operation was under way. Among the most sought-after items were cougar pelts: warm, soft, prized for their even color, but maneless. American Indians gathered from throughout the New World to trade and sell the bounties of their land to the Dutch West India Company. Europeans and early white settlers, familiar only with the maned skins of African lions, forever asked their indigenous trading partners, Why don't you ever bring us male pelts? Amused by the whites' ignorance of the New World's fauna—male

1

cougars, after all, have no mane—the American Indians explained with great emphasis that the male cats were so savage, so inaccessible, that they only lived far, far away, hiding "in the mountains." And so it was that during my great-great-grandfather's life, the great cats that early white traders—suffering a joke at their own expense—called "mountain lion" still roamed this wilderness.

Fast forward to the twenty-first century: cougars, where they once were, are no more. The vast eastern portion of the United States and most of the Midwest share this in common with Sandy Hook—the lineage of the "panther" that may have chased my great-great-grandfather no longer roams these wooded glens. Where the Rocky Mountains meet the plains, from north to south along the eastern borders of Montana, Wyoming, Colorado, and New Mexico, cougars were triumphantly and unsparingly trapped, poisoned, shot, baited, hounded, and bounty-hunted from more than half their former U.S. range. Today, just fourteen of our forty-eight contiguous United States have sustaining populations of cougars.

Somewhat contradicting this fact, daily Google Alerts hail news to the contrary, that somewhere in the country where cougars are no longer believed to exist someone claims to have seen one. The media simplifies such random, mostly alleged sightings—in Arkansas, "Cougar Sighting Has White County Residents Scared" and "Panther Seen Near Plainview"; in Connecticut, "Neighbors Spooked by . . . Mountain Lion?"; in Illinois, "Is There a Cougar Among Us?" And then invariably come the sound bites from "experts" claiming that "cougars are expanding their range," when in fact what comes closer to the truth is that the great cats are likely attempting to recolonize areas they formerly called home. In these places cougars may be seeking, and finding, refuge where they may be less likely to have to negotiate the threat of sport-hunting or confront the equally deadly threat of another cougar, or where prey may be more plentiful.

GIVING VOICE TO COUGAR

This collection of essays and stories attempts to give voice to a controversial animal that few people have or ever will see. Each piece is introduced by a brief statement that does nothing more than hint at what you, the reader, will discover through these authors' eyes. Their experiences are diverse yet connected through the common denominator of *awe*. They come from varying backgrounds — some hunters; some academics, artists and poets, researchers; and some simply going about their lives — and are linked by an encounter with this great cat that has affected the way they view some facet of their lives. Their stories are a testimony to cougar's power, both symbolic and literal.

The book has been compiled in a way that one might experience a cougar in the wild. It is underscored by a hint of cougar's presence, a common vein that runs throughout the collection, echoing what a few may have felt or many may imagine feeling — that pulse of wildness while in the out-of-doors, the desire to see a cougar coupled with a fair dose of realistic hesitation about the possibilities of this actually happening ("In Absentia," "Lion Markers"). It may be that such a "sixth sense" leads to an encounter that, although not inherently threatening and perhaps even thrilling, gives way to the reality of dealing with a carnivore on your — or their — home turf. In "The Growl," "Lion Story," "Talking with a Cougar," and "A Lion, a Fox, and a Funeral," things begin to heat up and the authors' endorphins stir as they come face-to-face with cougar.

Sometimes such interactions prove enough to inspire a latent curiosity on the particulars of the species: its history, how and where it lives, what peoples revere it, what it hunts, and the kinds and functions of the landscapes it depends on to survive ("Sanctuary," "The Sacred Cat," "A Short, Unnatural History"). We are fortunate to have the voices of those whose dedication to better understanding this elusive species contributes to its long-term survival. Here, we learn about their work from the inside out; how these authors see, interpret, and react to the challenges that come from studying *Puma concolor* ("South Dakota Cougar," "A Puma's Journey").

Because the boundaries between myth and reality often run close and narrow, two stories speak to the darker side of popular lore in "Hunting at Night" and "Lion Heart." And since this animal, both historically and in the present time, is capable of touching our inner as well as outer lives, we've included pieces that incorporate the archetypal and psychological value of cougars, in dreamtime and beyond ("To Cry for Vision," "Border Cat," "My Bush Soul, the Mountain Lion," "The Shifting Light of Shadows"). Finally, no volume would be complete without those words that are nothing less than poetry and with their clear, precise beauty strike at our very core ("Closer," "Drought").

THE NATURAL HISTORY OF COUGAR

Before the widespread extirpation of cougars in the eastern United States in the late nineteenth and early twentieth centuries, these magnificent cats lived most everywhere throughout the Americas. But even though they were widespread, they were relatively few when compared to herds of herbivores like deer, elk, and bison. Cougars are a classic low-density species, meaning that a single animal needs around one hundred square miles to hunt, roam, and call its own. Males are staunch defenders of their territories whereas females, along with their offspring, are more tolerant of overlap from other family groups, allowing a male cougar to roam their territories for the chance to breed with them. When the time comes for cubs to leave their mothers, their goal is to establish territories of their own on land productive enough so that they may hunt their requisite one deer or elk approximately every week to ten days.

This proves a greater trial for male cougars. Sometimes, in an attempt to take over another male's territory, the two males may fight, often to the death, for the right to live in optimal habitat replete with prey or to mate with local females so that the victor might inject his genes into the pool of cougar DNA. The challenging male, if successful, may kill a mother cougar's kittens, who would otherwise remain in her charge until they reach an average age of eighteen months old. Oftentimes, the mother cougar also dies in the battle, trying to save her kittens from the harsh realities of natural order in the complex social structure of cougar life. Coined "intraspecific strife," this social mechanism executed by males within cougar ranks helps to keep their numbers in check. Ecologists and renowned researchers Ken Logan and Linda Sweanor, in their seminal book *Desert Puma*, cite that in their non-hunted study area little more than half — around 60 percent — of the kittens survived, a testimony to the tough life of a cougar.

Despite the many challenges cougars face in the wild, their first and foremost cause of mortality is due to humans and their whims: deadly roadways slicing through their territories and sport hunting. Even hobby animals — including smaller-scale domestic livestock like sheep, llamas, and goats, penned but not enclosed, free-ranging but unattended, captive yet not protected — can prove fatal for a cougar who is tempted by one of these easy targets. Depending on the attitude of the landowner, that cat may be taken out on what's called a depredation permit, basically a one-way ticket to death row by a hired gun and his team of dogs.

So who *is* this tawny tiger, this ghost cat, this "panther"? It is, first and foremost, powerful. It is silent. It is large: the smallest adult females weigh around ninety pounds and the largest Boone and Crockett trophy males will tip the scales at over two hundred pounds. It is solitary; only mothers raising cubs form solid family groups and then only for the first fourteen to twenty-two months of their kittens' lives. Cougars are capable of killing a 700-pound elk and skinning out a porcupine — though not without consequence. And since they are gifted with such extreme prowess, such extreme skill at stalk, ambush, and kill, yes, they can also kill a full-grown man.

When viewed in motion, a cougar runs with a rocking gesture to its gait, front paws striking the ground nearly in unison as the rear paws follow. Its tail — long, sometimes as long as its body, so thick it appears to challenge the girth of its neck — acts like a creature of its own volition, a rudder steering and offsetting the course of stocky, muscular legs and skillet-sized paws with claws like those of housecats, retracting to muffle its steps or flashing out to grasp its prey.

There is a painting by artist September Vhay that portrays a mule deer doe; her body is in profile, her stance interrupted by a sound coming from the woods. One ear is up, askew, as she probes the environment for any hint of danger, a warning sign that may save her life. This brief moment of awareness may be her last if that sound was made by a cougar.

We see this time and again in our lives, on television and often in real life: one being dies, giving another what it needs to survive. No animal evokes this sense of the cycle, this web of nature, on such a grand scale as the cougar. Awesome they are, and no matter how beautiful, they are not to be taken lightly.

Likewise, they are not as ferocious or as eager to attack humans as the rare news event may frighten us into believing. Shy and with-drawn, cougars are charged with the high task of surviving alone. Unlike wolves, they live completely on their own, without the support of a pack to care for their young and help make their kills. Pure carnivores, cougars are meat eaters by nature's obligation and so must live without the omnivorous options enjoyed by bears, who are able to survive on roots, berries, pine nuts, and shoots with only the occasional dose of pure protein thrown in when opportune.

What has helped craft the narrative of fear surrounding cougar has also allowed this animal to survive, resulting in a fate far better than that of its fellow carnivores: wolves were eradicated and grizzly bears persecuted to the point of earning a place on the list of Endangered Species. Cougars are masters of landscape and can adapt to the rugged isolation of high mountain cliffs or the slimmer pickings of a remote desert habitat. Prairies are no more a challenge than any other place, with riverways and stands of deciduous trees where deer may take shelter, where cougar can wait at meadow's edge, crouched in grasses, not unlike the lion of Africa's savannas. What more could we expect from *Puma concolor,* the "cat of one color," which was once the largest ranging mammal in the Western Hemisphere?

This ability to adapt and to blend in is reinforced by a schedule that falls during the crepuscular hours of sunrise and sunset. The first word used in a scientific text to describe the species is *cryptic*: infrequently seen, this cat is even rarer a danger. It is aston-ishing, really, that more people have not come into contact with cougars considering this statistic: eight cougars have been collared and tracked in the Santa Monica Mountains since 2002. A conservative estimate of visitors to the state park is around six million people *per year.* Amazingly, not more than a handful of visitors have reported seeing these feline residents. And at that, many of the reported sightings were not cougars, according to scientists, but dogs, coyotes, and even housecats masquerading in the imaginations of those viewers as these stellar carnivores so many people simultaneously would love, yet dread, to see.

Cougars can powerfully call forth our innermost fears because it is on this very edge that cougars reside in our psyches, straddling both fear and awe. We want to see one — even just a glimpse, just once — yet we don't want to be confronted with a situation outside our control. But rarely are encounters with cougars on human terms.

In the United States, thirty-two people died by dog bite or attack in 2003 alone and around twenty people per year die of bee stings, versus the twenty cougar-caused deaths since 1900 (see table, p. 176). Cougars draw our interest and spark the imagination just as their presence is capable of quailing even the most seasoned outdoorsmen, the most rational of individuals. Some written accounts capitalize on this primal need to recognize that which can hurt us, to call it out of the dark. Often, the efforts result in a sensationalized view of a creature who is simply trying to survive, to hold its place in the world among habitats that are increasingly fragmented, degraded, or inhabited by humans. Teddy Roosevelt said it best — about ten years before my great-great-grandfather was reportedly "chased by a panther" — when he observed, "No American beast has been the subject of so much loose writing or of such wild fables as the cougar."

Roosevelt's critique reminds me of the power of story, and the need for us — as a civilization and as a community — to hold our stories, to keep them alive through their telling. At no previous time has *Puma concolor* needed its stories to be told as much as right now.

LISTENING TO COUGAR

Cougar cries have been likened to a woman screaming or sometimes a baby crying, a sound described as both haunting and haunted, a primal wail that settles into a place that exists within us and that we know to avoid; a sound that awakens a deeper and older side of our humanity, calling forth the instincts of our cavemen predecessors and their ability to survive, relying primarily on instinct. To listen to a cougar is to feel what it means to be *wild*.

In this sound are the beauty and the reminder that we are rarely alone in the wild. And when we most think we are is likely the time when we most owe it to ourselves, and the wild, to know better. Having traveled much of the world, I find there are few countries more gifted with wild places than the United States. An admirable history of conservation—although one not immune to criticism—has mostly protected tens of thousands of acres of land from the fingerprint of humankind. In places like Yellowstone, practically my backyard, one sees this immediately. Leave behind the busy park roads and concession stands and within a half hour you find yourself in some of the rawest, most unbridled backcountry—complete with the full complement of wildlife—in a matter of minutes.

But with cougar, we don't always have to go there. More and more, the wild *is* a part of many people's backyards; we have come to it, and it, having nowhere else to go, has stayed. Now it rubs up against new tract-home developments and the peaceful promise of suburban and rural life, where so many people are seeking refuge from the chaos of other people, traffic, pollution, and noise. In these cases, as more and more people close in on the realm of wildlife, especially large obligate carnivores like cougars, public awareness, coupled with human tolerance and a conscious effort to prevent encounters, may be this species' only hope for long-term survival.* Their future rests in human hands.

As with wildlife in general and carnivores in particular, the stakes run as high as the emotions generated by their presence: Will these big cats still be around fifty, one hundred years from now? Will there still be self-sustaining populations of cougars, or will there be only a few random sightings here and there, with some people

---

* Cougar safety tips can be found in the back of this book.

trying to prove — while others aim to disprove — cougar's existence, as is now the case in the Midwest and the eastern United States? Or will the United States more closely resemble the European Union, with our states so fragmented by human settlement that large carnivores simply have no place left to roam?

The players in this game are made up of a diverse rubric of stakeholders: those invested in conservation, wildlife management, science, stockgrowing, and the enduring livelihood of their families; hunters with their preferred pastimes; urban refugees with second or retirement homes in the New West and other areas; those concerned with ethical issues surrounding wildlife and dedicated to animals and their existence as sentient beings in their own right; and more.

In such a climate, the boundaries become blurred. Oftentimes wildlife management veers from doing what is scientifically sound, or prudent, and wanders into the arena of making decisions not principally based on conservation but more heavily on perception, politics, and, most always, the almighty dollar. But the problem begins behind the scenes, with statutes in place that hog-tie many state agencies to depend solely on money generated from hunting licenses. The problem with this bureaucratic business model is that each year, fewer and fewer Americans hunt — already the statistic holds at around a paltry 3 percent. Even so, with the proliferation of media networks broadcasting animal stories 24/7 coupled with an increased awareness of and care for animals overall, more and more people are interested: in animals, their welfare, and in how well state agency professionals may, or may not, be doing their jobs. It is hard to place blame on the increasingly outdated culture of wildlife management, whose origins grew from, and whose efforts have historically been funded by, the "hook and bullet" constituency, those who literally consume wildlife, be they hunters or fishermen.

At The Cougar Fund, members of the public sometimes contact us because they are concerned about the hunting and pursuit of cougars with dogs for sport. We regularly hear, "I hate and disagree with cougar hunting! Why don't you just buy all the cougar tags?!" But the issue there—besides ostracizing those who do hold a place at the table, no matter where one's ethics lie—is that cougar tags are sold in *unlimited* quantities although for meager sums between $5 and $30 for state resident tags. The stopgap measure for actually killing "too many" cats is set by a quota limit determined by state wildlife agencies and their governing commissioners: political appointees, most of whom have little to no expertise in biology or conservation.

A more thoughtful model might involve decreasing the number of cougar tags sold but increasing their cost. Most people who want to kill a cougar hire a professional outfitter to take them to find the cat, and that person will get paid anywhere from $2,000 to $6,000. The financial benefit the state game agency reaps then is only a small fraction of the hunters' total dollars spent—from 0.08 to 1.5 percent of the outfitter's fee. This is a pathetic amount, really, considering that the cougar is a rare and enigmatic big game species almost always hunted to provide a trophy.

On the other hand, houndsmen—people who train their dogs to scent-track certain animals, especially cougars—have proved surprising allies in the goal to bring better and more sound science to setting cougar kill quotas. In the purest sense of hounding, the entire activity could be compared to a much larger version of catch-and-release fishing. The cougar is tracked and then treed by dogs. The houndsman may photograph the animal and then call off his dogs and go home for the day. Does the cougar experience stress? Most certainly, just as a housecat would if it were chased by a neighbor's dog. But much of the time with hounding, the cougar is not shot, and although kittens may sometimes be mauled, they are less likely to be orphaned, the hierarchical male territorial society is usually not affected, and the greater cougar gene pool is not shortchanged by the loss of one of its individuals. Of course many times houndsmen do contract out as outfitters and will guide hunters, who will kill the cougar, but this is the easiest part of the "hunt" and anyone who has seen a cougar being shot out of a tree understands this (killing treed cougars has been likened to "shooting fish in a barrel").

In 2000, when Tom Mangelsen and I met with the representative from the Northern Wyoming Houndsmen Association, we compared notes and discovered that we were calling for four out of five of the same things, beginning with strict female subquotas, or caps, to prevent the unintentional orphaning of dependent cougar kittens. Winter 2007 found a similar alliance formed among Colorado conservation groups, including Sinapu and houndsmen's organizations. Emulating Montana's hunter education program to train outdoorsmen to distinguish between grizzly and black bears, the Colorado Division of Wildlife amended their hunting regulations to include mandatory testing of prospective hunters, who must be able to distinguish male from female cougars. These kinds of changes are occurring as the interest and engagement of the general public increases, and with state game agencies accountable, they understand that few people will tolerate orphaned young being left behind by irresponsible policies and practices that may not only compromise the health of a species, but further damage the general public's perception of hunting.

When it comes to cougars, or any species, the current game management setup provides little opportunity for financial contribution and, thus, buy-in by the non-hunting public. The architecture in most states for an average person sympathetic to any given animal and interested in donating money simply does not exist. Instead, these people look for an outlet that will specifically benefit the species they are concerned about (which is how and why The Cougar Fund came into existence—with stakeholders who found themselves voiceless and disenfranchised by the current management of *Puma concolor*). Most venues to support state game agencies come in the form of hunting tags; buy a tag and it counts as a vote for the consumptive—versus conservative—use of wildlife. Likewise, those consumptive users—hunters—are quick to remind the non-consumptive public that they "pay for wildlife." And it is difficult, after all, to find a way to charge a bird-watcher or nature photographer or hiker to pay for something that they don't technically take with them. What may help, then, is a rebranding effort on the part of these state game agencies to include all stakeholders with the goal to generate a more dependable revenue stream and better funding for both the animals and the state game professionals who are charged with their conservation. No small feat, to be certain.

Today, much has been accomplished but much remains at stake. A friend of mine remarked that refocusing state game agencies' priorities on science is tantamount to moving glaciers. True progress, like anything of value, takes time. Wyoming, although still concerned with maximizing hunting opportunities, researched and implemented a mountain lion management plan that is based on landscape ecological models, including the idea that habitats that generate wildlife (source areas) may compensate for less productive habitats (sink areas). But as my coeditor, Marc, frequently points out in his talks around the world, "Science is not value free." My home state, Wyoming, serves as an excellent example of how professional and personal agendas and biases inform the implementation of wildlife management programs. Recently in Teton County, in spite of sound and quantifiable biological evidence conducted independently of the Wyoming Game and Fish Department that a certain Hunt Area 2 is producing no female recruits to the cougar population—they are simply being killed, or dying, too fast—both the department biologists and the governing body, the Wyoming Game and Fish Commission, suggested and approved continuing with the liberal hunting program that is adversely affecting the area's cougars. This point is especially worrisome given that females are considered the "biological savings account" of any wildlife population. To make matters worse, Teton County's governor-appointed commissioner further shunned sound science by appealing, unsuccessfully, to his fellow commissioners to double kill quotas in an adjacent connected area and to do away with the few protections female cougars in the area are given in the form of subquotas. This Wyoming case is a classic example of the clash between facts and values, and what still occurs in spite of a populace largely made up of well-educated citizens who grasp the important role of carnivores in ecosystems.

Of course, scientists, policy makers, politicians, special interest and animal rights' groups, and wildlife bureaucrats will continue to debate whether any animal needs to be "managed," along with whether management equals conservation. In the meantime, those who care about wildlife, regardless of their values, are coming closer and closer to arriving at the crucial common ground necessary to make sure this elusive but important predator sticks around into the next century and beyond.

At the end of the day, the question is not whether to hunt — the old arguments for or against have little to do with cougar's long-term survival when we, as a society, have the proverbial bigger fish to fry of rapidly diminishing habitat and vanishing wild corridors coupled with attitudes that may or may not be tolerant to the presence of the big cats. One hundred years ago my great-great-grandfather probably couldn't imagine that the wild panther might not survive the twenty-first century.

So now, on behalf of our contributors' efforts to shed more light on and bring more awareness to the animal we fondly refer to as America's Greatest Cat, Marc and I invite you to read and enjoy *Listening to Cougar*.

IN ABSENTIA

Wyoming — A lone ski into Wyoming's backcountry yields evidence that a cougar plies the wild, in the author's midst.

Heading across the lake this morning — Jackson Lake — breaking trail through a foot of new snow. Out here on the ice, a mile from either shore, the world seems polar: an empty white plain under a great blue sky. Without trees or any other reference point, I feel diminished and exposed. I give my ski pole a tap on the ice. Yep, solid. It should be. It's been cold for days. Still, I pan my eyes ahead, looking for telltale dark spots that will indicate upwelling water. Carefully, but full of excitement, I go on, angling toward Ranger Peak, its 3,000-foot-long northeast ridge sweeping elegantly from summit to lakeshore. It's a line that I've coveted for quite a while, not only for its beauty but also because it's doubtful that there'll be another track on it. The long approach, the dangers of the ice, and the remoteness of the northern Tetons in winter turn most skiers back.

On the far shore, I ski up the bank and cross what would be boggy meadows in the summer. Now, it's a field of undulating

15

snow hummocks. Down into Colter Creek I slide, its water buried deep beneath drifts, and skin up the other side, onto a slope of adolescent lodgepole growing back after the fire of a few years ago. Up I continue, connecting shallow benches through the steep slopes so as to reduce the avalanche danger. Finally, I emerge onto the northeast ridge itself. There's a big meadow up here, and then a run of spruce and fir that merges into an ascending grove of aspen trees, their white trunks honey-colored in the low sun.

Around my boots, the feathery hoarfrost makes a whispering sound, and, knowing that the skiing will be quite good on the descent, I take a route along the edge of the trees, leaving the center of the glades untracked. Where the aspen turn back to conifers and, at last the open slopes of the upper mountain, the snow also changes. It's wind-hammered and hard, and I put on ski crampons to climb it. Shortly, the runnelled snow turns into sastrugi — gnarled fingers of bony snow that point like dead hands downwind. On the summit ridge itself, the snow has been transformed into alpine ice that wends its way around rocky towers and scree.

Then there's no place left to go. I take off my skis, sit on my pack, and drink some tea while looking at the big view — the Wind Rivers, the Absarokas, and the Tetons curving away to the horizon. There's also the sweet sound of nothing — just sky and rock and ice. After a few more minutes of listening to the emptiness, I put on my pack and reverse the route, weaving through the sastrugi with care and being just as careful on the bowl of bulletproof snow. It's not a place to fall. The aspen glades are better than I had hoped — perfect reconstituted powder and hoarfrost rushing dryly around my shins. I drop off the north side of the ridge and after a dozen turns stop abruptly above a line of cliffs. There's a clear shot through them, but the open slopes below are very steep and have avalanche written all over them. I climb back up and descend through the conifers — much safer. Back I swoop through the young lodgepole and into Colter Creek itself.

And there, crossing my tracks of just two hours before is the track of a mountain lion. There has been hardly any sign of life in this winter fastness — no grouse tracks, no weasel prints, only the faint tracery of tiny mouse feet. And here's this lion — its track bold and unmistakable, each round print a couple of inches wider than my palm and a little bit higher. A big male cougar.

Looking right, I can see his line of tracks stretching all the way down to the lakeshore, along which he has walked, giving anyone skiing across the lake a long and vivid sighting. But, of course, there's not a soul on the lake, and I wonder if he waited until after I ascended the ridge to expose himself. I have a feeling that this is exactly what he did, for cougars are cautious beings. In fact, during the nearly four decades that I've roamed the Rockies and Andes, I've seen just five of them, four at the same time on the National Wildlife Refuge — the famous mother and her three kittens who, denning close to the road one winter, thrilled thousands of viewers. The fifth cougar whom I've managed to spy was in Yellowstone National Park, and the sighting took place in the last light of a June dusk. Even through my spotting scope, I wasn't sure if the animal lying under a faraway spruce tree was a cat or a chimera. Yet, despite my never having had what I call a "wild sighting" of a cougar, I never fail to keep a lookout for them — searching the hillsides, sitting in likely locations, and waiting . . . waiting. And what I've gotten for my efforts is this — the cougar in absentia, its tracks appearing from nowhere and vanishing into nothing, with only a haunting vibrancy in the air indicating that I am being watched. It's been frustrating, and not for me alone.

For a moment, I recall my dog Merle's similar frustration with cougars. A half-wild pup whom I met in the Utah desert, Merle was mostly Lab, with some Redbone Coonhound thrown in, and knew all the wild animals of our region well. In fact, his body language when he encountered their spoor was a clear indication of how he felt about them. Of coyotes he remained forever disdainful. He'd prod their turds apart with his front paw — always the right one — then give it a quick shot of pee, a scrape, a grin, a rapid "ha-ha-ha" pant, and move on.

With wolves he wasn't so casual. Encountering their scat, he'd take it apart with the same poking motion of his paw that he used with coyote sign, but after a single sniff, his face would fill with deep consideration. No grin, no pant, no pee, no condescension. He'd give me a sidelong glance from under his brows: "Yes, the big dog has stood here."

If he'd come across the ropy pies of grizzly bear, he'd take a deep, shuddering breath, finishing with a tremor at the bottom of the intake. A very slow and steady look around the forest would follow — almost always we found grizzly scat in the forest — his eyes calm but watchful. He'd give a small, respectful wag of his tail. "The great shambling one. Let's watch our step." With black bear, he'd give no more than several quick snorts, a little poke with his claws to reveal half digested fruit, followed by an offhanded grin. "The little bear. Maybe we'll see him. Not to worry. No trouble here."

The round prints of cougar, however, sent him into cascades of baffled inhalations: "What is this? What is this? What is this?" It was the only creature of our homeplace whose spoor he smelled frequently without seeing the animal itself. Of course, he recognized that cougar odor resembled the odor of domestic cats, one of whom we lived with. Yet there must have been orders of magnitude difference between the two. Merle's concentration over lion spoor reminded me of a scholar poring over a fragile manuscript, written in a language barely discernible to him, the ancient roots of the words familiar, the grammar almost parsable, but the meaning — a physical shape for the animal — just beyond his grasp. Merle would go down the trail with his brow furrowed, his nose returning again and again to the track.

Now — following Merle's lead — I put my nose into one of the lion's prints, but not being a dog (a creature whose nose is about forty times more acute than that of a human) I can only catch the scent of fresh clean snow. Glancing up, I see the lion's tracks tracing the smooth undulations of the drifts. It appears that he was playing on this winter roller coaster and even appreciating the up-and-down design of the drifts, for there are places where he went deliberately uphill to follow their crest instead of taking the more economical line of travel beside the creek.

For a moment, I try to place myself in his mind. I doubt he was hunting. No deer or elk live up here at this time of year — the snow is too deep for them and there's nothing to eat. Nor is there any sign of moose. In fact, all the willow stands that they might browse are completely covered by snow. I wonder if he has simply been taking a walkabout: out for an afternoon's cruise, just exploring and having fun, as am I. I hope he is. Of all the fellow travelers with whom I would care to share this winter silence, he is at the head of my list. I'd love to see him, but I know, hermit that he is, he wouldn't care to be followed.

Turning my skis downhill, I descend along his tracks, making turns along the crest of the drifts and stopping here and there to search the cliffs above. Who knows—I might catch a glimpse of him. But, as usual, he's nowhere to be seen. Down, down I continue, pausing occasionally to glance over my shoulder, still hoping to see him, but also being cautious. After all, even though he's a lion who appears to have an aesthetic appreciation of winter, he's still a lion. And I'm just about the right size for dinner.

THE GROWL

Oregon — An unexpected feline visitor creates a stir among a cabin's owners. Pondering what to do, the couple considers calling the officials.

The growling I heard from under the cabin was something new; something deep and, well, scary, like deep animal growls are supposed to be. It was dark, New Year's Day, and we'd just gotten back from a week-long holiday absence.

One of our dogs was sticking his snout under the cabin, an eight-by-ten-foot outbuilding I use as an office, and barking intently. I knew right away that something was under there—the dog was acting unusual. I hadn't even gone in the house yet, which is of course all one wants to do after traveling cross-country for the day, but I had to investigate, see what was there, and at least get the dog to simmer down.

Just thirty feet from the house, the cabin's a log timbered structure with open alcoves under the flooring, the early-winter snow already piling up around it and the nearby pines.

As I crunched through the snow I casually assumed that I'd encounter the neighbor's cat hunkered under the structure, being unnecessarily intimidated by the dog, or maybe a raccoon, which the dogs hate for some reason and can't resist a good barking session over.

"OK, buddy," I said, exhausted. "That's enough. Let's see whatcha got under there . . ." I tapped the dog and he quickly trotted behind me, and I took another step, approaching the opening under the shack. That's when the growls struck my ears and I came to a complete stop. I remember hovering there for a moment, half bent over, one hand on the side of the cabin, about to fully bend down and peer under the structure, when I was forced to pause. I've thought over this moment time and time again.

How does one describe this sound? "Deep and guttural," although a cliché, seems fitting. "Sepulchral" is even appropriate, although may be too much of a negative connotation. The intensity and volume of the growl, a booming, disturbed purr, told me that I had to immediately upgrade my idea that it was just my neighbor's cat under the cabin.

As a naturalist I've frequently lectured kids about animal interactions in the natural world, about how the size of a particular species is often irrelevant when it comes to intimidation. "Aggressiveness is the key to intimidation—often independent of size." Many a small songbird chases a much larger hawk out of its territory simply through displaying aggression. Often, it's not worth it for the hawk to expend the energy to fight back. Animals have countless forms of bodily display: bold markings, postures, ear flares, squints, hisses, honks, and growls—that's their vocabulary when it comes to intraspecies communication. These are not necessarily predator-prey interactions; these are more likely territorial emotions conducted to simply express "Back off."

As I hesitated outside the cabin on that frosty night, half-hunched over, ready to peer into the unknown, I was confronted by an auditory "Back off!" I don't remember feeling fear, I really don't recall being disturbed, only I knew that I had disturbed something else.

I needed a flashlight. I was elated as I high-stepped back to the house. The dogs were waiting a few dozen feet behind me and it wasn't until much later that I realized how unnerved they were. The barking directed under the cabin was, I believe, much for show and ceremonial territoriality, perhaps mostly to let us humans know what was in their yard (i.e., their "territory"). But when I was trotting back toward the house, the dogs seemed pleased to be heading back toward sanctuary.

At this point I was considering which animal I might possibly be dealing with. I was thinking bear, with an outside chance of cougar and the possibility of a big, stray dog. Hmm. Just a dog would be disappointing.

I quickly crashed through the door, all three dogs bursting in with me, and momentarily made eye contact with my wife as I snatched the flashlight off the wall. She looked up from the stack of mail: "What's going on out there?" With a wry smile and arched eyebrow I stated, "There's something under the cabin," and bolted back out the door. She came right behind me, descending the stairs in the frozen snow. "Whaddya think it is?"

"Don't know. But it's big."

I thumped toward the cabin, perhaps too quickly, almost afraid that what I knew would be an epic natural-history sighting might have left, and was pleased to hear the growl return as I approached.

Darkness was deepening as I clicked on the light. I squatted and spun my arm toward the opening. Face-to-face with a brown animal. A big, brown cat. It bared its teeth and hissed to greet me. I didn't feel fear. It was nestled too deeply in a tight place, unable to lunge. It was apparent that the cat was terrified and it didn't move.

I knew it was a cougar. But still my scientific mind had taught me that I needed to prove that it wasn't *not* a cougar. So I just stared, squatting, holding the flashlight before me, flipping through mammal field guides in the margins of my mind.

Uniform brown face with dark cheeks. Ear tufts? No. Tail? Can't see. White chin? Roger that. Paws? Can only see one and it's pretty damn big. Cat size? Well . . . it's kind of small, like a medium-sized dog, a small Lab, for example. So I kept flipping back and forth between cougar and bobcat possibilities, but I knew it was a cougar. It struck me as a young cat—immature. So I wondered if a young bobcat would have ear tufts. But, if this was a bobcat, it was really big.

That white chin—that was the clincher. When it comes to big cats, I was lucky enough to have seen one years before.

On a wet spring evening I was heading uphill into the pines and foothills of the Cascades where I live. The trees were sparsely scattered with lots of manzanita, bitterbrush, and other shrubs hugging the sides of the road. Suddenly, about two hundred feet in front of me, a large mule deer doe popped into view, bouncing across the road. She was trotting rapidly in a diagonal direction away from me. Deer are common in the area and one comes to expect seeing them in winter and spring, but something felt different about this sighting.

I had frequently commented how the local deer population was very car-savvy. They'd see or hear vehicles coming and calmly step away from the pavement a few feet, then return to the roadside grasses before your taillights faded. But the deer on this particular night was bouncing recklessly in front of me. My foot was already coming down on the brake, slowing steadily. Where you see one deer, there are usually more. That's when I saw the next one coming hard in the corner of my eye. Much closer than the first, it was bounding through the underbrush right at me. I was decelerating rapidly but I was sure that it and my van were on a collision course.

At that moment my memories are chilled into slow motion. My gaze shifted off the road to the right where the animal was just bursting into view. The van brakes groaned and the engine whined, slowing. The brown shape cleared the brush, landing less than ten feet in front of me. I was going to hit it. Its head turned, shocked by my vehicle's appearance, and I met its disturbed, angry glare over the corner of the hood. My vision defied reality. For one instant, burned into my mind as my headlights lit up the cat, I made eye contact with the ultimate ghost of the mountains. Its eyes shone like fire, ears flattened, giant whiskers flared outward, white chin clenched, and muscles rippling down from its shoulders to its massive feet.

In full sprint, the cougar's front paws hit the shoulder of the road when its gaze spun toward me. At that moment, I swear that its rear legs were still moving forward when the front legs recoiled and the entire animal sprang backward. The van jerked to a stop. I peered through the passenger window to where the cat had been, seeing only leaves of manzanita and darkness.

"Oh my God!" I heard myself say. Still staring, my mind couldn't catch up with what I'd just seen. My first thought—and I'm not making this up—was "Someone's pet African lion has escaped." The cougar was huge. I believe that its head, from the base of the neck to the tip of its nose, was fully eighteen inches long, bigger than any dog I'd ever seen.

I looked back to the left where the deer pounded away into freedom, realizing that I'd inadvertently saved its life, and I stared back to where the mountain lion had disappeared. The smile must've gradually crept across my face as I realized what I'd seen and how lucky I'd been. I never expected to see a cougar. Although I'd spent a lot of time in backcountry situations where I knew the cats lived, I still never thought I'd be so fortunate as to spot one. That sighting left me feeling giddy for days.

The vivid memories of that frozen moment surged back through my mind as I stared at the frightened young cat in front of me. Its growls and snarls were an obvious weak attempt to deter me. Its body never moved and it was apparent that this cat wasn't about to leave its shelter.

"Honey," my wife finally asked emphatically, "what is it?"

It occurred to me that my answer would have some shock value and I considered tempering it somehow, but I just nodded and coolly stated, "There's a cougar under here."

Immediately, she was backpedaling, heading for the house, spouting at me, "Get outta there!"

"No. It's OK." I backed off, wanting to give the cat some space. "It's young, one or two years old." I looked over at my wife, smiling, and beckoned her. "C'mere. It's pretty cute."

It was. The cougar was likely in its first winter away from its mother and still had some distinct kittenish looks to it, albeit very large ones. We took turns looking at the cat from a respectable distance for a few minutes and then, once darkness was complete, we made our way into the house.

Then we had a dilemma. What to do? We felt obliged to make some phone calls to the immediate neighbors and encourage them to keep their pets indoors for the night. But what to do with the cat? Should we have it removed?

Because it was New Year's Day and after 5:00 P.M., there wasn't an agency — state, federal, or local — available for advice, so my wife wound up on the phone with the Oregon State Troopers, informing them of the situation. They said they'd get back to us.

I'm sure that it took several minutes for our adrenaline to diminish, and after we discussed the situation in detail and considered all of the possible consequences, we realized what we were invoking.

"The State Troopers don't have wildlife considerations to make," I mentioned, "other than whether or not this animal is considered 'a threat.'"

My wife looked at me inquiringly.

I continued, "If they come out here, they're gonna kill it."

She immediately got back on the phone, was told that a deputy was on the way, and after asking the dispatcher what the plan would be, was informed that the cougar would likely "be destroyed."

Now, I have no complaint with the state police, but at that moment I became quite defensive of the young cat under the shed. We know that we live in cougar country. Our property is surrounded by national forest land and the area is rich in scenery and wildlife. That's why we live here. We knew that this cat was innocent of any wrongdoing and deserved a chance to make it on his own. We determined that we'd simply wait until morning and hopefully, by then, the underside of the cabin would be vacant.

Unfortunately, the next day, we were shocked to learn that our fuzzy friend was still entrenched in his temporary home. Now we had to confront the issue in the clarifying details of daylight. We liked the fact that the big cat had dropped by, but we didn't want to actually live with it. He'd likely had a recent big meal, and it was probable that the cat was planning on sitting comfortably in such a sheltered, dry place for the next few days. He was certainly a threat to our own housecats, maybe our dogs — enough to make me glance over my shoulder occasionally for many weeks to come.

We were determined that we would scare him out. This was silly, but fun. We invited some friends over and we all pranced around the yard, whooping and clanging pots and pans together. In hindsight, I realize how senseless this was. The cougar was comfortable under the cabin. There was no way he was coming out to encounter that ruckus.

Eventually, we quieted down, piled up snow on one side of the cabin, which left him only one exit, and slowly prodded him through the snow with a long section of plastic pipe. We all stayed on one side of the cabin, giving the cat free and unintimidating access out to the other side.

From the house, my wife said, "He's coming out." We kept prodding. Then we heard, "He's out!" and we all froze.

Looking around the side of the cabin, I saw the young mountain lion slowly padding through the hard snow into the shelter of the pines. He never looked back, just kept trotting, perhaps hoping that no one would notice his departure. I stood there, just a few feet away, keenly observing the animal. I had a camera in my hands, but I didn't want to interrupt my view of a young cougar stealing through my yard. His coat was thick, well insulated, but still bore the spots a young cat relies on for camouflage. I'd guess that the cat was between fifty and sixty pounds. He made it to the trees, turned this way then the other, before I lost sight of his long, thick tail, and he was gone.

We've told this story over and over since it occurred three years ago. When I relate the details of this experience, people simply listen, jaws open, studying my words, wishing they had been there. The impact is the same no matter who the audience: people are mesmerized by mountain lions, and I feel fortunate to be the teller of such a tale.

The next day after that young cat padded away I followed his tracks. Along with a couple of friends on snowshoes, we followed them for two or three miles, losing and then regaining the trail. The tracks wandered in and out of forested areas, along the edge of a large creek, and then simply disappeared.

We stood there at the edge of the creek, looking across, even up, wondering if it could have made a jump in any particular direction. But it was clear that we were off the trail, the cougar was again alone, and we were all more fortunate for the experience.

LION MARKERS

New Mexico – Originally published in 1928 in Country Gentlemen *magazine, this account of cougar hunting captures the nostalgia of technology-free lion pursuit, a rarity in modern-day hunting.*

Way high up in the Mogollons,
Among the mountain tops,
A lion cleaned a yearling's bones
And licked his thankful chops.

That is where Paul Bransom and I went to hunt the mountain lion—the American lion, the Mexican lion, the panther, the painter, the puma, or whatever other name one wished to bestow upon the cougar species of the cat family. Westerners generally refer to him as mountain lion, or simply as lion. Texans nearly always call him panther, and panther is the word, with its corruption painter, that connotes the great hunters of old days, like Daniel Boone and Davy Crockett. Some people call him catamount, but the catamount proper is the wildcat, or lynx. I propose to use whatever name sounds best in the place and at the time it is used.

Eighty-five miles by automobile from Magdalena, New Mexico, across the winter-browned Plains of San Agustín, then to the road's end in the Black Range, and we were at the Evans brothers' Slash Ranch at Beaverhead. Twenty miles with pack mules over a trail of Datil National Forest, and we were at the Horse Camp on the Middle Prong of the Gila River, perhaps the best mountain lion country left in the United States.

Formerly the panther ranged over entire North America, but a lion country nowadays must be inaccessible. Inaccessibility means brush and rocks and a country that is rough. The forks of the Gila, with their intersecting canyons, are as rough as a million years of ice and snow and rain and wind and sun and volcanoes—ages ago extinct—can make and unmake, scar and weather the rocks.

It is the malpais, "bad country." Here are mountains covered with pine, spruce, and fir and fringed with manzanita and stubborn shinnery. Here are slopes and plains dotted with alligator junipers and sweet-nut-bearing piñons. Here are wide mesas of grama grass, and moating the mesas are canyons that cut down a sheer thousand feet—Jordan, Cassidy, House Log, Brother West, Indian, Panther, Butcher Knife, and many a lesser.

Finally, a lion country must be prolific of lion food. The lion's staff of life is deer meat. He likes turkeys, and there are plenty of turkeys in the Mogollons. He licks his chops over antelope and beaver, both of which survive in numbers along the Gila. Frequently, other food being scarce, he kills calves and yearlings, but seldom does he bother cattle in the Datil National Forest.

He grows fatter on colts and mules than on anything else, but horse raising is pretty much an obsolete business now. All he asks is venison, and anywhere on the upper forks of the Gila venison may be had for the asking. Every day we rode I saw forty or fifty deer.

But even in the best lion country rigid requirements are necessary for catching a lion. The requirements are trained hunters, trained dogs, and, generally, persistence and endurance. Lions are shy and wily creatures. Men who have hunted them a lifetime and have killed scores of them have told me that they never saw one until after he had been jumped by dogs.

The Evans brothers, Dub and Joe, are certainly experienced hunters. Seventy-five years ago their grandfather was ranching and hunting in southwest Texas. Nearly fifty years ago their father pioneered into the Davis Mountains, on the western edge of Texas, where the lion and the Apache had for ages held possession.

By the time Joe and Dub were ten years old they were running *ladino* ("wild") Longhorns and following the hounds. In a single year they helped catch fifteen lions out of the canyon on which the Evans home ranch was established—Panther Canyon, it is called. Altogether they have caught hundreds of lions. In the few years they have ranched in New Mexico they have caught thirty-three. They're what the Mexicans call *hombres del campo*—"men of the camp."

As for their dogs, there is not a better pack in Texas and New Mexico. The family of hounds of which they are the latest generation has been with the Evans men for thirty-nine years. When a year old, the original pair of pups, Belle and Brownie, began hunting lion and bear and soon developed into remarkable dogs. By line breeding, with an occasional cross with bloodhound and Redbone hound, the characteristics of old Brownie and Belle have been strictly preserved.

The original names pass down from generation to generation. Today the leader of the pack is Brownie, mighty of foot and mouth and muscle, as confident of himself in the field as Nelson at the Battle of Trafalgar. As good and more energetic is Belle, beautifully spotted and amiable of disposition. Then there are Short Brownie, Little Brownie, Francis, Trumm, and Lee Wilson.

The older dogs never notice the tracks of deer, coons, coyotes, foxes, and the like. They will take a wildcat's track, but are easily called off it. The only animals they really hunt—and, once they have struck the trail of, follow despite hell and high water—are lions and bears. Our hunt was at a time when most bears have gone to sleep for the winter.

The moon was yet shining, the thermometer was at zero, and the dogs were comfortably filled with the flesh of a slaughtered mare when we struck out across Black Mountain the first day of our hunt. About noon, as we were riding down in the very bottom of a deep canyon, the dogs opened up, but the trail soon proved old. After much searching Dub Evans made out two lion tracks, one of a full-grown lion going down the canyon, the other of a young lion going up; neither track fresh enough to follow.

We went on, the dogs smelling at the foot of trees and nosing along the base of boulders and palisades. The lion likes to walk on a narrow bench under bluffs. He likes to cross rough saddles, or dips, between highlands. He likes to prowl the length of narrow hogbacks that look down into chasms on either side. He likes to meander along projections and indentations of a naked rimrock, following the ragged edge sometimes for miles.

Brownie and Belle and their followers knew all this. They never failed to examine any log so fallen that there was space between it and the ground. The lion likes to walk under such logs, bow up his back and rub it like a cat. If a twig bent over the trail, the dogs sniffed it, for the lion often leaves the scent of his body or tail on weeds and bushes.

We were topping out of Brother West Canyon when the dogs opened cry with immense energy.

"Sounds good but not very fresh," remarked Dub.

The trail followed over a malpais ridge. Once in a while the dogs would lose it for several minutes at a time. Then Brownie or Belle would pick it up. There was no soil for the track to show in. It was the kind of country that a lion feels safe in traversing, for the lion depends on sight more than on any other sense. He sees everything, and he thinks that if he leaves no visible impressions, he is safe from pursuers. Sometimes while prowling over the country he winds about in all sorts of ways, apparently for no other reason than to keep rocks under his feet.

How dogs can smell where a padded foot stepped on a rock perhaps forty-eight hours before is truly marvelous.

"Over yonder is the canyon of Indian Creek," Dub said.

Beyond the blue vacancy I saw a line of cliffs. Suddenly the dogs stiffened their tails, stretched out their heads, worked their noses, let out a long and peculiar bay, and were gone. "They have smelled a kill!" said Evans.

We followed at hot speed. Presently we came upon the dogs tearing at barren deer bones over which no lion would ever again lick his "thankful chops." The ribs were still red with dried blood, but they had been picked several days before.

The kill was under a gnarled juniper tree on a shelf of rocks overlooking the junction of Indian and the Middle Prong of the Gila. The bark of the juniper was scratched with lion claws.

Spread out below us, like the ruins of some incomprehensible and fantastic mammoth, was a skeleton world over which the hounds of the elements had gnawed and snarled for dizzy aeons. The dried and scattered ribs of the skeleton were cones of rock, red and yellow and gray. The twisted and broken legs were ridges of wrecked boulders. The grave of the skeleton was walled in with cliffs that only an eagle could surmount. If it was not the Grand Canyon, it was a grand canyon. On the point of an escarpment I saw a blotch of red. It was possible to work one's way out to it. The blotch proved to be a bone of the lion-killed deer.

"The raven we just saw put it there, I guess," said Dub. "Always watch for ravens. They locate the kills every time."

We had trailed a lion either to or from the kill, we did not know which. It was entirely possible that we had back trailed. Certainly it was an old track to an old kill. The dogs seemed unable to work away.

"Lead my horse around to yonder point," said Dub, "and I will take the dogs and skirt over some of those ridges below us."

He pointed to a saddle half a mile around the head of a side canyon.

When, an hour later, he came up without having discovered a sign, the sun was far down. Camp was six or eight miles away. Before we headed for it I looked back. It was a magnificent, an ideal lion country, and we had little doubt that a lion was in it within finding distance. During the night he might, out of idle curiosity, pass the abandoned kill. We would come back in the morning.

Dawn found us, Indian file, rimming out of the deep canyon in which we were camped.

As we topped out onto a mesa the dogs took an east-by-north course instead of our intended east-by-south direction. But the

Evans boys refused to change them. Luck, destiny, providence, something might be directing them. We were outward-bound, bound to get a lion. The fact had as well be told. We did not strike even an old trail that day. We cut for sign over some of the ground we had traversed the day before, but the dogs were too intelligent to take up again a trail they had worked on and abandoned.

The next day bore the same lack of luck and the next and the next. We scouted east and west, north and south. It snowed, rained a little, and the southern slopes melted. It snowed again, and the northern slopes were as slick and hard as glass. We slid down those slopes into warm, deep canyons and somehow wound and climbed out of them.

Often we were afoot leading our horses. I discovered that by grasping the tail of the horse in front of me as we plodded upward I could get my wind and my footing with much less heaviness.

Those mountain horses climb like Rocky Mountain sheep and are as fearless as rock squirrels. They went up desolate steeps that would literally pen in to death and starvation a trainload of plains horses. I would not have traded my mount, Insect, for the finest stabled steed in Newport.

One day we saw an eagle maneuvering to catch a fawn. Another day we let the dogs tree a wildcat. On the iciest, shadiest, roughest slope in Catron County we found where a huge black bear had spent a week not long before. Flocks of piñon jays jeered at us. Tassel-eared squirrels played bopeep from the branches of great pines. We saw more deer than cattle, mule deer and whitetails both. Often we looked eagerly at ravens, but the fact that ravens locate a panther kill does not mean that every raven denotes one.

Up at four o'clock in the morning. Before dawn a hot and meaty breakfast, saddles, and the clear bugling of a hunting horn. Some raisins and nuts in the pocket to munch on for lunch. Hours and hours of riding and hoping and looking. Such was the order of the day for three, four, five, six days. On one of those days, Sunday, it was snowing, and we rested ourselves and the dogs. The Evans boys don't hunt on Sunday anyhow.

And the shadows of evening always found us back at the Horse Camp, ravenous, tired, every fiber in the body yearning for hot food and a roaring fire.

How much hot beefsteak one man can eat I do not know, but had a weigher been present at the Horse Camp any night we were there, he might have found out. Plenty of meat, plenty of tobacco, gallons of coffee, forests of pitch pine to burn, a snug cabin, company immensely congenial, grain for horses and mare meat for the dogs—what better camp could a man ask for?

The two log rooms and open hall of the cabin, unfurnished though they might appear to some eyes, contain a hundred details that cry out stories and character.

Where the puncheons, countertops, about the stove in the kitchen have decayed from water, heat, and salty grease, they are carpeted with cowhides. The chuck box—ponderous, iron-braced, the lid lined with copper—used to be the combination box and seat of the Silver City–Magdalena stage. The hooks on the walls are old horseshoes and eagle talons. On one log a bear's foot is tacked. On another place a pair of eagle wings are stretched. Ancient elk horns are hung and thrown here and there.

Out in the hall, brass cartridge shells stud the ends of logs. The door into the bunk room shows a storied bullet hole. The logs about the same door and next to the great fireplace are burned and carved with cattle brands.

Never was there a better camp for the spinning of yarns than the Horse Camp. The winter nights in New Mexico are long, long nights, and Joe Evans is one of the best storytellers west of the Pecos. In the lore of American animals the bear has no doubt figured as the subject for more tall tales than any other beast, but the panther, particularly in the Southwest, has provoked more strange stories.

So when the talk turned to panthers, as it did hour after hour, night after night, we could all help Joe along. How lions kill, how they cover their kills, their strength, their size, their disposition to travel, their scream, their fear of man, their ferocity, their playfulness, their patience, their markers—every phase of lion nature we discussed and yarned over.

We must have talked more about panther kills than about any other feature of the great cat. We were hunting all the time for kills. If we could find a fresh kill, we were reasonably certain of jumping the killer. He might stay away from it for a night, but the chances were ninety to ten that he would return the next night, eat, leave a fresh trail, and be lying up somewhere near when the dogs were turned loose in the vicinity at dawn.

The lion is more prodigal of meat than any other predatory animal. Sometimes he slays merely for exercise or nothing more than a drink of blood from the jugular of his victim. At the same time, in the care of his meat he is probably the most intelligent and meticulous animal in the world. He likes his meat fresh and clean.

As soon as he makes a kill, he removes the entrails from his prey. Unlike the wolf, he begins eating on the foreparts of an animal. If the place at which he has slain a buck or other game does not suit him, he carries it to a proper place. Then he carefully covers it with leaves and twigs.

And so the nights passed, with talking on many things really, but never long off the subject of lions and lion dogs and lion hunts. One night we settled the mooted business of panther screams. They do scream, although seldom, and sometimes in a blood-curdling note, the testimony of certain hunters to the contrary. And the days passed with hunting. It was the morning of the seventh day and we called it good.

We were down in House Log Canyon. About ten o'clock Brownie let out a bellow, Belle sent up a cry, and the other dogs turned loose a varied and stirring noise that sent the blood tingling to the roots of our hair.

"Lion sign and no fooling," said Dub as I rode up to where he had already dismounted at the root of a pine. The dogs were slowly working away up the canyon.

"I've been telling you about lion markers," Dub went on. "I never saw one in Texas, but New Mexico and Arizona lions make them all the time. Here they are. Some hunters call 'em scratches."

What we were looking at were parallel scrapes on the ground about eight inches long, at the base of them a little mound of pine needles. They had evidently been made by the lion with his claws hooded. Double up your fists, dig them down into leaf mold or pine needles, draw them back to you at one stroke about eight inches long, and the result will be something very much like a lion's marker. The little ridge between where the lion's hooded paws have scraped in parallel lines always shows.

As the lion rakes back toward his body, a marker always indicates in what direction he is going, whether any tracks are visible or not. Of course the markers remain for weeks after tracks have vanished. Only males make them.

For an hour or more we worked up the canyon, so slowly that most of the time we were on foot, trying to help the dogs with the trail.

"Look here," called Dub, who had followed the dogs to a bench fifty feet above our heads.

He had found another marker made in gravel against the bluff.

The trail finally climbed out of the canyon and struck across a lava mesa. It came to a kind of barren place with not a twig or a blade of grass to hold the lion smell. It took us an hour to go less than half a mile.

"Just as well pull for the top of that mountain," said Dub. "Once a lion starts up a mountain, he is going to the top."

When we struck the southern slope, where the snow had all melted and run over the tracks, we were absolutely stalled. We were a day too late, and the day's work was about over. People don't hunt mountain lions at night as they do coons. According to the course he was taking, the lion was making for the very broken country along the Middle Fork between Indian and Butcher Knife canyons. We had not yet been in that territory. We headed for camp, determined on the morrow to hunt out the promise.

On the trail in, Dub told me a remarkable story about lion markers. A year or more ago a government hunter in the Middle Gila country got on the trail of two lions, a male and a female. He followed them for two days, camping out both nights without food. On the third day he caught the female lion; then, seeing nothing of the male, he went on into camp.

Two weeks later while riding after cattle Dub struck a fresh kill made by a male lion. He knew the lion was a male from the markers right at the kill. It was in the country the government man had hunted over.

Dub went to the ranch, got his dogs, and was at the kill early next morning. He had no trouble in striking a good trail, but the lion was not lying up to digest food. He was roving, day as well as night.

Over Black Mountain and down into the canyon country, Dub followed the trail at a good gait all day long. And every little distance he found a lion marker. He is sure that he found a hundred markers, all made in one day's time. The lion was putting out sign for his mate. He was searching the country for her.

Late in the evening the dogs jumped him, and even after he was jumped he made a marker—a very, very unusual act. After Dub killed him he cut him open. There was not a bit of food inside him. He had been too desolate to eat.

When the morning of the eighth day dawned the world was white with fresh snow.

Hardly a quarter of a mile from the camp the dogs opened up on a hot trail. Joe and Dub called them off without even looking at the trail. What the dogs said to them was "wildcat."

Well, the day closed, the magazines of our saddle guns were as full of cartridges and our hands were as empty as they had been for a week. We were thoroughly disgusted with the Middle Fork and all its eastern tributaries. The lions might be on the other side of Gila. They were not on our side, for certain. They might be ten miles away, and ten miles of canyons that include the Gila River in the Mogollon Mountains is as far as two hundred on pavement.

Our plan was to leave very early the next morning without packs, but carrying on our saddles a ration of grain for the horses, some mare meat for the dogs, and coffee, bread, and meat for ourselves. We would cross the Gila and let luck direct us.

We wound headlong down Meadow Trail, worked around cold bluffs for an hour, and then headed up Fiddler Trail for the land of luck.

It must have been about two o'clock when we struck a fresh kill. It was a ten-point white-tailed buck. One forequarter was gone and the tongue eaten out.

There were two or three markers under the trees about it.

"We've got a check and all we have to do is cash it," I yelled.

"Wait," said Dub.

"Just wait," said Joe.

It happened that the kill was on a mountainside where very little snow had fallen, but there were plenty of rocks and timber. Before we had time to do anything the dogs were coursing off at a lively rate. If a lion has smeared blood, the contents of a deer's entrails, or other fresh animal matter on his paws, he leaves a trail that can for many hours be scented at a long run. The way our dogs were making tracks indicated that they were on an outgoing trail made by lion feet well smeared.

Still, there is only one sure way for a man to know whether his dogs are going with tracks or are back trailing. That is to see the tracks. The blindness of dogs to tracks is as remarkable as their acuteness in smelling them. Some hunters say that if dogs go faster uphill than downhill over a trail, the chances are that they are back trailing, the explanation being that lions in going downhill put more weight on their feet and therefore leave a stronger impression than when climbing. However that may be, the only sure way of telling an out-trail from an in-trail is to look at the tracks. Our dogs were going fast enough downhill.

We followed them, now galloping, now pausing, looking all the while for tracks. Joe discovered a track, but the impression was so light that it was impossible to tell which way it was pointed. Unless the ground is soft the knobs on a lion's heel sometimes look almost like toes.

When we came to where the dogs had crossed a gulch in the bottom of which was sand, the tracks were plain. We were back trailing.

There was nothing to do but call the dogs off and return to the kill for a fresh start. Quickly the eager dogs found another track that we made sure was outgoing.

It went down into rough country, and it was as tortuous as a corkscrew. The dogs came to bluffs over which they had to be lifted. Even if a lion were jumped there, he stood a good chance of getting away. With night about to close down it was folly to trail farther.

"It's only about a mile from here to a spring in Little Bear Canyon," said Dub. "I packed some deer hunters into that place a month ago. A quarter of a mile above the spring I saw a cave. We'll spend the night there."

Dogs, horses, and men were all glad when we struck the soft bottom of Little Bear. At the camp we found a side of deer ribs that the hunters had left and that a month of cold weather had not injured.

When I fed the dogs I noticed for the first time that their noses were bloody raw. No wonder! Those noses had been without let, grazing over malpais rocks by the tens of thousands and poking under acres of snow, snuffing, snuffing for lion sight. Galley slaves never worked harder than those dogs worked for us. They were used to sleeping out, but when we found a place for them in one corner of the long cave before which we built two fires, they were very grateful. The pleasure in seeing them warm was about the only pleasure I realized that night.

We discussed an Indian proverb, then each man made himself a wallow. The Indian, according to tradition, said: "White man heap fool. Build big fire and have to stay long way off. Burn and freeze. Indian wise man. Build little fire. Stay close to it. Warm." We had a saddle blanket apiece, we kept on our overcoats, we replenished the big fires at least every forty minutes. I am inclined to think that the Indian was right.

With the first light we saddled. A short hour's ride and we were at the kill. The lion had been there during the night, although it was apparent that he had not eaten more meat than he could well carry. He might be lying down within a hundred yards, or he might be off at some distance. We took his trail at a gallop. It made for the rough canyon we had quitted the evening before.

As the dogs struck the canyon rim they all at once hushed, apparently nonplused. Dub and Joe were down on their knees, working like dogs themselves.

It took ten minutes to discover that the lion had leaped from the rim into a juniper tree which grew out of the canyon wall, had climbed out on a limb of the tree, and then dropped off under the rimrock. A lion does not often play fox tricks.

As the dogs with a joyful bound again took off, we remained on top where we could hear and see and come as near being with the dogs as we could be anywhere.

They followed down the canyon under the rimrock on our side, crossed, and began working back up the canyon on the other side. Above them towered an uneven wall of rock that could be scaled only at intervals.

"Look at old Brownie in that grass over yonder," said Joe. "Acts as if he were hunting rabbits."

A tolerant grunt at the joke was all the response that Dub gave.

All of us could see Brownie, though nobody had seen him climb out. The other dogs were still under the bluffs. Brownie was at least two hundred yards out from the canyon rim on a smooth mesa. Between him and the canyon was growth of scattered cedar.

"Look! Look!"

It was the first time I had seen Dub excited.

"I caught a glimpse of a panther in that cedar. I'll swear I did."

Nobody else saw a panther in the cedar, but what we all saw a minute later was a long, tawny form gliding through the grass away from the canyon of barking dogs and toward silent Brownie.

With the corner of my eye I saw Belle about to climb out.

The tawny form was gliding, drifting, moving like an effortless ghost straight toward Brownie. And Brownie had turned and was coming in a long run back toward the canyon and the lion.

In mid-prairie they met.

It is a mystery of nature why such a powerful and lethal fighter as the mountain lion will run from a dog. But run he will invariably.

The lion we saw wheeled like a released bowstring. I would not attempt to say how high or how far he jumped. As he whirled and leaped the slant morning sun showed his breast dazzling white.

When he reached the canyon rim he was at the climax of his speed and he never checked a second but spread himself flat like a flying squirrel for the awful leap. It was a hundred and twenty-five or a hundred and fifty feet to the first bench below, but the space was not altogether clear. Some rocky spires jagged up part of the way.

With outstretched paws the lion caught one spire, swinging himself a quarter around and slightly breaking his fall. A second rock he barely scraped.

While he was making that leap I do not think that one of us drew breath. By the time he hit, Brownie and Belle on the rim above were simply having fits.

It was a lucky thing that the younger dogs had not topped out. One of them must have seen the lion leap. In a minute's time they were in full blast behind him. The race could not last much longer now. With long tail straight up over his back, the lion was doing his best but was plainly flagging.

Directly he came to a series of rocks that ran out at right angles to the main canyon wall and sloped sharply up. He ran out on them, leaping over a little gap that the dogs could negotiate. On a pillar-like abutment he halted. Far above him Brownie and Belle, who had kept up with the race, hung their heads over and cried. Below him the other dogs gave the cry of conquerors. He was bayed.

When we got down to him he was still panting hard. He lashed his tail and opened his mouth and spit. He seemed to consider trying another desperate leap.

He was game and noble game, the noblest and the most beautiful predatory animal on the American continent. As a bullet found its mark I felt, momentarily, mean and ignoble. I shall never forget him. That last bit of chase, that leap, the fervor of the dogs, the tawny bundle of cornered killer up there on the pillar of rock were worth all the ten days of grueling work we had put in.

When the lion's body fell to the ground and we examined it, we found that all the claws of his right paw had been pulled out by the clasp he gave the rock that checked his fall. One claw on the left paw was out. But he did not have a bone broken.

He measured eight feet and six inches from tip to tip.

BORDER CAT

*Arizona – Border Patrol agents, immigrants, and a wild puma
unknowingly commingle on a harsh desert landscape, each of them
aiming to avert the eyes of the next.*

The female puma sleeps in a dense thicket of mesquite and acacia trees. Songbirds and owls occupy the branches above, while a rattlesnake lies curled up in a pile of rocks close by. Flies find the moisture hidden in the puma's nostrils. As her body twitches, her ears funnel sound to her brain relaying information about her surroundings. The breaking of branches and heavy shuffling of feet disrupt the puma's dream. She lifts a heavy eyelid and waits. Fifty yards from her day bed figures are seeking shade from the noon sun. They are loud and clumsy with their movements. The puma raises her head and watches. What she witnesses is not new to her. This disturbance is becoming more and more common in her daily existence.

Four people find refuge in the shade of a large ash tree. They are sweaty and tired, gulping dirty water from their half full milk jugs. They speak in soft tones and look over their surroundings. The puma can smell their fear.

The first time the puma encountered humans she was intrigued with their awkward movements. She had followed the people as they walked a desert path. Their two feet scraped and stumbled under them while their arms swung and flailed in an opposing movement. The creatures fumbled so much as they moved across the terrain that they appeared to be injured. They were also loud, emitting noises constantly, and they sounded like they were both dying and claiming their territory at the same time. There were loud huffs, high-pitched squeals, guttural screams, and low moans.

The puma's stealth and awareness allowed her to go unde-tected during her investigation. Her tawny body blended in with the land, vegetation, and rocks but the people stood out in their bright and dark skins. She was able to get close enough to smell the creatures. She memorized their scent. The puma grew leery of the two-legged creatures as she followed in their footsteps. Then, her instincts warned her to back away from their proximity. The puma's curiosity was satisfied. The beings were not prey, and couldn't be a predator. That was all that mattered.

Later, once again, the puma watches the two-legged creatures. This time from a distance.

Suddenly, something new happens; the strange beings begin to run. The puma's ears prick up and her body tenses. There is a new sound entering the area and the two-legged creatures seem to be afraid of it. A loud rumbling comes toward the puma with the speed of an antelope, yet it remains hidden. The earth swirls and sprays about as a new creature emerges. Standing in the wide sandy wash that is a part of her home is a large, shiny being. It dwarfs any prey that she has encountered and has eyes that flash and its body is the color of danger, white.

The puma remains in her bed, hidden but agitated. Her heart rate accelerates and her wiry body pulls taut. She is ready to explode from her spot and flee if discovered. She looks upon the new creature as a possible competitor. The puma keeps her ears tuned to the rocks falling from the hillside where the two-legged creatures have gone and holds her eyes on the new creature.

Suddenly, the creature opens up and more two-legged beings emerge. They are of a different, uniform color, but have the same scent. The new versions of the two-legged beings chase after the others up the slopes that border the wash. They are just as slow and clumsy and make the same huffing sound, but also growl a bit. The chase goes on for a few moments and then a loud thumping sound is heard in the sky. The air above the puma's head moves as if a storm is approaching. Her hair lifts from her body just as magnet shavings respond to metal, giving her the appearance of a cat before a fight.

It is too much for the puma. She springs from her position, leaping over the fifteen-foot arroyo and sprinting up the opposite hillside until her heart can take no more. Atop the ridge, the puma keeps a vigil over her lands until the chase of the two-legged creatures is over. She doesn't have to wait long. The ones of the same color catch the others. Their technique is weak, even their pouncing on their prey is awkward. One misses. There is some struggle, but then the attack is over. The air goes calm and soft noises drift to the puma as the two-legged beings pace back to the large white creature. All beings are still alive—perhaps they were playing a game like she does with her prey on occasion? But then, the large creature swallows the two-legged ones. Death has finally come and the large being leaves her lands.

The puma turns east and follows a game trail to another section of her territory. She will never return to this wash again.

A PUMA'S JOURNEY

New Mexico — More than a decade spent studying cougars reveals the many trials and tribulations of adolescent males as they venture out and attempt to establish territories of their own.

The doe behaved oddly. She stopped foraging and cautiously walked toward a small thicket of junipers. At about forty meters, she stopped and stretched her neck forward, as if straining to see or smell more clearly. Still appearing unsure, she began to circumnavigate the thicket. When her circuit was almost completed, a young puma broke from the cover. He trotted fifteen meters away from the deer, stopped, turned, and returned to the thicket. Thirty seconds later, the puma reappeared and bolted upslope to a lone juniper a stone's throw from his initial hiding place. Although the young cat did not use characteristic stealth, the doe's gaze remained fixed on the thicket. She finally lost interest and began feeding. After a quiet hour, I realized the doe and her comrades — a loose group of does, fawns, and one fork-antlered buck — were working their way toward me. Since I did not want to become part of this interaction, I cautiously moved down the draw and off Antelope Hill. No matter. Despite these efforts, my careful movements were more distracting than those of a flustered puma; I was acknowledged by quickly raised heads and frozen stares. To my relief, I proved even less impressive than the cat—the deer resumed feeding. I fixed my binoculars on the lone juniper. If the deer had detected me, surely so had the puma. I smiled when I saw him. This time he used all available cover to his advantage and returned to his original hiding place. His tawny coat blended well with the sandy slopes, but I caught the flash of a yellow ear tag and the black collar around his neck. I knew I would have to return to this place, just to see what Kidd, as I called him, thought was so special about those two little juniper trees.

We first caught Kidd in the summer of 1989. Tracks indicated a female and her two cubs were using Black Mountain and traveling the desert draws that led up its south side, including Bonney Spring Canyon. Black Mountain is at the southern end of the San Andres Mountains, located in south-central New Mexico. This long, narrow range stretches seventy miles from south to north, rising up slowly from the creosote flats on the west and dropping dramatically to the desert floor—a mix of Chihuahua desert, gypsum sands, and ancient lava flows—to the east. Although the mountains may appear barren from a distance, the view is deceiving. Perennial springs bubble up through limestone rock and form pools along stretches of shadowed canyons, helping to sustain a rich assemblage of plant and animal life. The tallest peaks reach high enough to break the desert's grip, supporting healthy groves of piñon, oak, and even ponderosa pine. Although the creation of White Sands Missile Range in the 1940s restricted subsequent human access and impacts on the land, the mountains are rich in human history. During our everyday activities we were reminded of its past—the pictographs, pottery shards, and grinding holes made by ancient peoples; the rock battlements where Chief Victorio and his band of Apaches once took refuge from the U.S. Cavalry; the crumbling walls of a stone cabin where it's rumored Billy the Kidd once hid; the abandoned homes of homesteaders, including one of lawman Pat Garrett, along with the corrals and pens used to house their

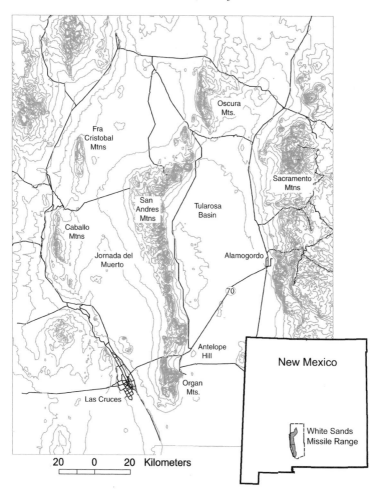

goats, sheep, and cattle; and the mine tailings and shafts from an era of frenzied mineral extraction. Now this place, with its relative isolation, limited human access, restrictions on domestic stock, and protected populations of pumas and their prey, had become an ideal location for a puma study.

That summer day, our team was nearing the end of the fourth year of a ten-year study of puma ecology and behavior; Kidd would be our sixty-fourth puma capture. As we approached, we saw a cat that was scared, defiant, and hot. A leg-hold snare held tight to his right forefoot. At six months and twenty kilograms, Kidd was still very dependent on his mother, Two-Catch (female #60), and would be for another seven months. Using a jab stick, we gave Kidd a dose of immobilizing drug. Once he was tractable, we removed the snare, recorded his vitals, and fitted him with an expandable radio collar. As he recovered from the drug, Kidd greedily lapped up water from my cupped hand.

Radio collars provide information on puma behavior and movements that cannot be gathered any other way. The only reason I got a glimpse of Kidd that day on Antelope Hill was that the radio-telemetry signal from his collar told me to look for him there. By radio-collaring pumas as cubs, we are able to determine who survives, who dies and from what, when they become independent from their mothers, and how they behave after independence, including their dispersal paths and distances. Such information can be vital to the successful management and conservation of the species.

The right environmental conditions, a mother's skill, the cub's good sense, and a healthy dose of good luck all play a role in a cub's survival to independence. Although newly independent pumas of both sexes undergo many survival challenges, this story focuses on young males. Newly independent male pumas have a strong urge to travel. Whether aggressive, territorial adult males instigate dispersal or it is more deeply programmed in the cat's genetics, these felid teenagers typically travel over one hundred kilometers from their birth site before establishing a territory of their own. Two of the longest documented dispersal distances were by males that left their natal areas in central Wyoming and the Black Hills of South Dakota and died in central Colorado and Oklahoma, distances of 480 and 960 kilometers, respectively. Such long dispersal movements by males (females that disperse typically move less than half the distance of males, and some females remain near where they were born) suggest it may be a mechanism to minimize breeding between closely related individuals.

That's the big picture. Individually, young males have many choices to make and challenges to meet. Two days after seeing Kidd on Antelope Hill, I returned to the site. Kidd was not there, but I did find out what was so special under those two juniper trees — the remains of an old buck and Kidd's first documented mule deer kill since independence from Two-Catch. Although independent, Kidd had not yet made any long-distance dispersal moves. His kill was at the south edge of his natal range, just south of the highway that connects Las Cruces with the headquarters of White Sands Missile Range, Holoman Air Force Base, and Alamogordo. We found that it often took males a little time before they dispersed, and sometimes they made several attempts (i.e., they would leave their natal area only to return days or weeks later) before they fully committed themselves. Kidd may have needed the prodding from a territorial male to finally make that move. Unfortunately, the male he faced gave no quarter. I was radio-tracking pumas from the air the day I picked up a worrisome double beat from Kidd's transmitter. I radioed Ken Logan (our field research leader and also my husband) with the news and met him at the site after landing. Male #88, a recent immigrant weighing sixty kilograms, had apparently discovered one of Kidd's deer kills. At fourteen and a half months and forty-two kilograms (even with a belly full of deer meat), Kidd was no match for #88. We found him lying twenty meters from the deer cache, puma hair in his claws and deadly bite marks to his head.

Most male pumas that survive to independence also survive long enough to begin their dispersal journey. But the path to a new home and a coveted territory is not an easy one. During the window of time we studied the San Andres pumas, larger male pumas killed more of the tagged dispersers as they ventured from their natal homes. Competition between male pumas for space and, more importantly, for the chance to breed with females is probably the impetus for the sometimes deadly fights between males. Such aggressive tactics have probably worked well for the species overall, allowing bigger, stronger, more experienced males to maintain territories where their offspring can safely grow to independence. But deadly fights are not the only danger young males face. Because of their inexperience, and possibly because they are more likely to take chances—it's a teenager thing—young pumas sometimes get into trouble with people or do things we deem undesirable. For example, after dispersing south within the San Andres Mountains, M23 began to settle into an area that supported some of the few remaining desert bighorn sheep on the mountain. He managed to kill three before a decision was made to move him to central New Mexico, far from desert sheep country. Another disperser (#92) traveled over one hundred kilometers northeast to private ranch-land where he was killed by the landowner for killing calves.

Probably because much of southern New Mexico has a sparse human population, none of our dispersing pumas had direct conflicts with people. But given the distances that these cats typically travel, it is not hard to understand why, in more populated areas, young cats—frequently footloose, naïve males—are sometimes found wandering through a residential area or up on someone's back porch, testing the palatability of the resident cocker spaniel. In general, the dispersing pumas we studied tended to follow the north-south axis of the San Andres Mountains, enjoying the security it offered for as long as possible.

However, dispersers sometimes made marathon movements across the wide desert basins. It appeared as if they were simply trying to get to other mountain ranges they spied in the distance. Although it may not be easy to trek through arid flatlands sparsely populated with anything a puma would find desirable to eat, imagine instead a puma trying to disperse through landscapes characterized by human development—perhaps along the Front Range of Colorado, from the Sandia Mountains east of Albuquerque, or through the Peninsular Ranges of southern California.

In 2025, eleven western states (Arizona, California, Colorado, Idaho, Montana, Nevada, New Mexico, Oregon, Utah, Washington, and Wyoming) will support about twenty-five million more people than they did in 1999. This population surge will undoubtedly create more challenges for dispersing pumas as more of their habitat becomes altered and fragmented. Although male dispersal is natural and beneficial to puma populations, it sometimes proves difficult and, on rare occasions, it fails to take place at all. Often this is correlated with human-caused alterations to the landscape.

In a study population in southern California, all male progeny attempted dispersal, but whenever they approached the wildland-urban interface, they stopped — at least for a while. One even returned to establish a territory adjacent to his natal area. The biologist studying that population concluded that unless habitat connectivity was maintained to allow pumas to move freely between habitat patches in the region, the puma population there would probably go extinct. In Florida, extensive agricultural and urban development has isolated the puma population and essentially prohibited most males from freely dispersing.

We even began to see glimpses of this problem in our study population, with the widening of the highway between the San Andres Mountains and the Organ Mountains to the south. Prior to the widening, adults and dispersers occasionally, and safely, crossed the highway. Kidd was among them. After the widening, we documented only two crossings, and both cats were killed. Dispersal is healthy for puma populations, allowing for the influx of new genetic material and repopulation of areas that have experienced extirpation or high puma mortality. Where human impacts affect puma movements, puma subpopulations will become less resilient.

In the ten years we studied pumas in the San Andres Mountains, we captured and tagged 163 pumas while they were still spotted, blue-eyed, nursing cubs. Of those, about 100 pumas made it to independence. The transition from independence to adulthood was tougher on the males, since about 44 percent of males, compared to only about 22 percent of females, did not make it. We recaptured any male that remained within the San Andres Mountains and survived into adulthood. However, we were unable to track very many of the males that ventured beyond the San Andres Mountains because either they were not radio-collared, they slipped their collars, or we lost track of them.

I was anxious to observe a success in the form of a male puma that dispersed outside the study area, established a territory, and produced offspring of his own. I thought I was going to witness it with Houdini, one of three cubs born to Female #4 in the summer of 1986. We marked his sisters at four weeks of age—but Houdini managed to evade capture (hence his name) until his first birthday. He stayed with his mother for two more months. When she met up with the resident male to breed again, Houdini was on his own. On the same hill where, over two years later, Kidd made his very first deer kill, Houdini found himself in a standoff with one of his mother's suitors—Male #1. Considering another young disperser had tried to evade #1's fury by climbing a utility pole (where he was immediately electrocuted), I was a little surprised—and admittedly elated—that Houdini survived the encounter. With experience comes wisdom, so I was not surprised when, days later, Houdini was on the move, traveling northwest across the creosote flats of the Jornada del Muerto (literally, "journey of death") to the Caballo and Fra Cristobal Mountains east of Elephant Butte Reservoir.

Weekly I would make the drive to the Alamogordo airport, strap antennas to the wing struts of a Cessna 182, and fly with pilot Bob Pavelka to locate pumas from the air. That's why I knew where to look for Houdini. Two days after one of these flights, I found myself negotiating the rutted dirt roads west of the reservoir, searching for tangible evidence of the cat. I stopped the truck by a shallow draw and poked along up it. There they were—the large, rounded tracks of a puma walking at a steady pace. I bent down and touched a track, and then gazed in the direction they headed—toward the dark silhouette of the Black Range. Houdini had safely crossed the Rio Grande and Interstate 25 and was heading to his new home.

This was the closest I would ever again be to Houdini. Over the next year I tracked him weekly from the air. Then we got the call—a hunter's dogs had cornered Houdini and he had been killed. At only thirty months of age, it was possible Houdini had sired a litter, but just as likely not.

It's hard to read success in the face of a frightened, narrow-faced, wide-eyed cat that is all ears. Number 82 (who would later earn the name of Lupe) had already left his mother and begun his southward dispersal move through the San Andres when we snared and collared him. At sixteen months and forty-three kilograms he was already bigger than many adult females, but he had the lanky look, narrow face, and flawless, tawny coat of a cat that had a lot of growing to do and experience to gain. Knowing the gauntlet of territorial males, busy highways, housing developments, hunters, and temptations (in the form of domestic livestock) Lupe would face once he left the San Andres Mountains, I was not optimistic he would live long. Maybe Lupe felt the same, since he soon turned around and went back home. Four months later he tried again, beginning one of the longest journeys of any of our tagged cubs. Lupe went south again, but this time he followed the mountain chain all the way to its conclusion, the Franklin Mountains overlooking the sprawling town of El Paso. For the next eighteen days, I could not find him. Then, with expanded aerial searches, I was able to pick up a familiar beat. Possibly thwarted by what he encountered, Lupe shunned the city, turned east, and crossed seventy-four kilometers of stark desert to a momentary safe haven in the Sacramento Mountains. His journey continued over the next three months, until something told him he had found what he was looking for—a new home in the Guadalupe Mountains.

Almost every week, Bob and I made the aerial journey to these mountains, searching for Lupe's signal. I still remember some of those trips—the contrast of white and wet gypsum sand on the wind-formed hills of White Sands National Monument; the rows of cotton-ball clouds below us, stretching to the horizon; the drone of the engine and hiss of the receiver as I strained to hear his signal; the drop in engine power and downward circling as we pinpointed Lupe's location in the rocky crags and juniper-covered hillsides.

A little over two years later, the batteries in Lupe's transmitter finally gave out; our connection was gone. But this time I was confident I'd witnessed success. Lupe was over four years old and a prime adult puma. Just maybe, one day, one of his descendants will make the journey back to the San Andres Mountains and his genes will again mix with those of the desert cats that dwelled there.

As a scientist I must remain objective; however, our intimate knowledge of these pumas' lives could not help but produce respect, admiration, and a pang of loss when an animal died. But the individual loss is buffered by the belief that the species will endure. I must also admit a bias, a deep desire for pumas to exist, to evolve, and to continue to affect the evolutionary direction of the ungulate species they depend on for survival. My experience with pumas in New Mexico leaves me hopeful; my further experience studying these cats in the rapidly changing landscapes of California makes me recognize the difficulties that lie ahead. Even on the Uncompahgre Plateau of Colorado, where I sometimes assist with monitoring collared cats, tagging cubs, and investigating the places where pumas have been, I can see the changes. In the summer of 2004, Ken and I stood on Horsefly Canyon's west rim and got tantalizing glimpses of puma #6 and his very vocal mate. Just above them, jutting from the opposite rim, perched a new two-story home.

Pumas are resilient and adaptable, but it will take a caring, engaged citizenship to ensure the puma's future. Part of our success will be dependent on a better understanding of puma behavior and not simply on our ability, or lack thereof, to precisely estimate puma numbers. Observing and analyzing the behavior of animals helps to inform us about the life history strategies that help them to survive, reproduce, and, ultimately, persist.

TO CRY FOR VISION

*Colorado – A series of meditative journeys in the wilderness – called
vision quests – exposes this author to the power of coming face-to-face
with cougar on the animal's terms. Inner growth is fueled as she learns
to face her deepest fears.*

My first awareness of cougar's power
came through the experience of another. Several women and I
gathered in late May in the Rockies outside of Lyons, Colorado, to
encounter our first modern version of a vision quest. Traditionally,
in many American Indian tribes, vision quests were reserved for
boys as they came of age. They were sent off alone to fast and pray
in the hope of receiving a vision in order to better understand their
place in the world. Today, there are spiritual teachers that allow
people to take part in a modified version of this experience in order
to clarify their purpose or deepen their connection to Spirit.

We began our experience on a 4,000-acre buffalo ranch, free
from any distractions except those we carried in our hearts and
minds. For the next four days our bodies would be free from food
and water as we nourished our Spirits with prayer and song inside
circles we marked with offerings to the Seven Directions — East,
South, West, North, Above, Below, and Within — to aid us on our

journey. Prior to going on our quest, we prepared offerings of herbs and prayers wrapped in cloth pouches that we tied to a cord. This cord of powerful intention would mark the perimeter of our circle. Our teacher would remain at base camp near the altar and sweat lodge. From there she would hold a strong connection to each of us by entering into a deep state of prayer and meditation. I had planned to set up my space down by the stream lined with old cottonwoods, but on my way there two rattlesnakes warned me away. I heard them before I saw them. The first one blended into the rocky path before me. I backed away slowly and found an alternate path further downstream, the coolness of the water calling me. Above the steady flow, I heard the second alarm; sharp, quick, and dry, the way I imagine a person's last breath would sound. Coiled and closer than the first one, I backed off slowly, gratefully putting more distance between my messengers and me.

Days later, I learned that the woman who chose that particular area beside the water encountered a cougar on her first night, just after dusk. According to her, it walked straight for her, stopped silently at the perimeter of her circle, and waited until she was no longer afraid. It sat there and waited. When she finally calmed herself, it walked off into the night. I remember hearing her story with equal amounts of awe and relief. I was amazed at her power and her ability to move through her fears, and relieved that it wasn't my story. That same night, high on the hill to the east of her encounter, I sat surrounded by buffalo mothers and their young bathed in the liquid mercury light of the full moon. My heart remembered a time when people and wildlife lived this way, in open expansive places, and I couldn't help but feel grief for so much of what we've lost.

Since I had committed to four consecutive quests, the next August found me in a wilderness area outside of Pine, west of Denver. One major difference was that there was no base camp, no teacher, and no other people out there with me. This time I was on my own. Because of this, I took a tent with me and enlisted the support of friends in Denver to hold me in the safety of their prayers over the next few days. I also asked my partner to come check on me the first night.

I set up my space in a small clearing in the woods not far from a stream. My tent was exposed, with some chokecherry bushes and scrub oak separating me from a stand of large ponderosa pines to the north. The stream trickled slowly in the west. A light, refreshing rain fell at sunset. I received it with gratitude as I watched the indigo clouds drape the western sky before I retreated into my tent for the night.

The first sound I heard after the rain stopped was the sharp crackling of sticks over by the stream. I thought it was my partner trying to find my site, so I opened the tent flap and called to him. The reply I received from the dark was a cougar's hissing growl broken only by the snapping of more kindling as it raced toward me. I froze for a second in the electric air before I jumped into the safety of my tent. The cougar slowed as it came closer, but it became more vocal as it circled me. Hissing first on one side, then the other, then around again. I crouched inside, turning with its voice. I felt as if I were prey, but the kind that couldn't flee, or fight. I froze again, tense with fear, not breathing, just waiting.

Somehow, I remembered the woman's story from the year before. I began to breathe. I used my breath and intention to channel my fear into the Earth. I exhaled fear, inhaled strength, over and over as the cougar circled. As I became calmer, the cat became quieter; its hisses farther apart. I wasn't exactly sure when it left, but I sensed its absence. Not too much later, the eastern side of my tent became illuminated as the full moon rose over the ridge. I stepped outside and let myself be embraced by its light. The air was still charged, but with power instead of fear. I stood in the silence, alert and alive.

My third quest took me back up north, on Colorado's Front Range, once again in August. Thankfully, I was in the company of others with our teacher at base camp. Just as I had each year, while preparing my prayer ties with tobacco offerings, I asked for the courage to free myself from fear so that I could live more fully. I set up my space on the side of the mountain, wrapping my ties around a strong ponderosa pine a few feet from the edge. Most of my circle consisted of an expansive rock lined with lichen that jutted out into the west-facing void. I sat in meditation that night, facing trees to the east. Just as I was focusing on my second chakra—the energy center in the belly that is typically associated with the color orange—I glimpsed the orange orb of the moon on the horizon. Simultaneously, a loud crack snapped my attention to my right. I stood and turned, my back braced against the pine tree just in time to see the cougar stop—only a few feet from my circle. We faced each other in the night. I continued to breathe, my muscles taut, obeying a memory beyond my control. Instinctively, I pulled my energy inward this time, containing it in my circle instead of projecting it toward the cougar. She responded with a sort of snort, a sound that resembled a chuckle, before she turned and walked away. I spent the rest of that night vacillating between wrestling with fear and praying for a way to finally let it go. The next afternoon brought three crows floating on thermals in the west. I saw the winds as a gift that could help me clear my clouded mind and heart, half of me anticipating another visit from the cougar. With every cell of my body, I breathed in the moist air as thunder bellowed in the canyon below. I let the storm receive all of my angst.

By the time the storm was spent, I was empty, totally open to what would come. Out of that space the idea of power coupled with gentleness was born. This became my intention for the nights ahead. Peace covered me like a soft, worn quilt and its warmth dried my damp, cold bones. It is hard to conjure an animal that embodies gentleness more than deer, which gifted me with their presence that night.

The cougar visited me one more time on that quest. It was our last night at base camp after coming out of our individual circles. I was in my tent working with my chakras again as lightning flashed outside when I felt her nearby. She seemed to come from the area where I had been sitting in my circle on the edge of the mountain. This time I was not afraid. Instead, I felt lighter than ever—as if I was literally plugged into her energy. Light began to fill the core of my body. It shifted in color from regal purple to pure white as it infused me completely before it spilled outward and spread throughout my tent. The prayer ties that surrounded me in my space for days were wrapped around a log on my lap. They, too, became illuminated and I felt the raw power of Spirit as I merged with its light. I knew in my core that I transcended the physical world and embodied the energy of cougar.

One year later, I had my last physical encounter with this magnificent cat. I was out with my teacher, but instead of holding base camp, she decided to sit in her own circle. We would go out as equals. My space was situated on the lower end of a sloped meadow with an ancient fir tree within it. The tree had been struck by lightning and now held my prayer ties around me. Exactly half of it was dead and charred while the other half was alive with soft green boughs that offered me shade. My companion was on the edge of the mountain, out of my line of vision. Later I learned that in the fading dusk, she had seen the cougar round the hillside before it began a quick descent into the meadow where I sat. Now in my sight, it pounced into the higher part of the meadow in front of me and ran from one end to the other, hissing and growling each time she struck the ground. I was reminded of my first encounter two years ago, yet I felt safer this time. My prayers came instantly, as automatic as my breath, each one punctuated by her growls. She didn't stay long, but the night did. I sat up against the tree and watched the full moon carry my shadow in an arc across the Earth in front of me.

I have been told that the animal that comes to you on a vision quest is your personal totem or guide, that it mirrors in some way your personal gifts, and that you have an obligation to carry those gifts into the world for the benefit of all relations. The vision that mountain lion gifted me with, repeatedly, is that of power. Carrying that vision involves embracing the power to live fully: to balance strength with gentleness, to walk in the darkness and emerge into the light. To realize that although true power is of the light, sometimes we need the darkness to find it.

At last, the moon began its descent as the dawn star rose. Hours — that seemed like days — later, first light slowly put the shadows to rest. Just as the clouds alit with pink, the cougar's screams pierced the eastern ridge. What I can best describe as a haunting combination of fox, crow, and a touch of human cry echoed through the canyon. The cat was moving quickly, farther away from two smaller cries that followed hers. It was then that I realized that she had cubs.

CLOSER

Idaho – This poet's experience with a cougar intensifies his already acute ways of seeing.

I had recently moved to northern Idaho to write, and everything I wrote was dull, forced, unnatural. One day I saw a cougar. He was easily eight feet, from his tawny head to the tip of his long tail lazily rising and falling, about the same size as the trophy cougar I once saw displayed in a glass box at a gas station down in Kamiah. He lay stretched out on pine needles on a slope forty yards away. I felt lucky to have seen him. I was also glad to be inside my house; we had come close enough.

The house I bought sits amid thousands of acres of timber in the Clearwater Mountains, high above the South Fork of the Clearwater River. The day after seeing the cougar, I decided to take down a hog-wire fence from a wooded area where the previous owners kept small livestock. I had no interest in raising anything there; I wanted what came forth on its own urges—deer, blackberries, turkeys, dogtooth violets—to have free play. Working around a thicket of wild roses to loosen the fence, I saw the bright carcass of a six-point buck. Something had been eating it. From the fresh scratch marks on a fallen larch holding up the buck's rack, I knew it was the cougar.

I once asked a forest ranger what I should do if I was ever surprised by one in the woods. "Likely the lion would see you first," he said. "And if he really wanted to jump you and break your neck, you'd probably never even feel it. Or," he added, "not long enough to worry about."

Charley Dreadfulwater, who has worked in these mountains for thirty years, helps me with chores I don't dare try on my own, like dropping big trees dangerously close to my barn. I told him about the kill. You don't know what to think about lions anymore, he said. "Used to be, you'd never see them, just their markings." "Now their fear seems to be gone. Last month, out after firewood, I had three of them not sixty feet away looking me over. Calm as anything. I eased back into my truck and waited for them to go away. I like lions. They were here first." He shook his head. "But there's only so much land."

A week later, I went to check on the kill. Only a rag of its fur, its bones and hooves remained. Charley told me that since I wasn't a hunter, which deer figure out pretty quickly, I'd always have plenty close by. And something to eat them. For several days, I avoided walking in the woods near dusk, when the cougar could see better than I could. But I kept staying out later and later, my neck aching from looking into low branches perfect for leaping from. Was I going crazy? Did I want to see a lion perched in a tree, waiting for me? Why didn't I at least buy a pistol?

One afternoon about a month later, I was in the corral, on my knees, pulling up thistles. The cold air was misty wet from a low cloud. I was trying to work off the bad feeling of having made mediocre sentences all morning. It seemed I was becoming an expert. I thought how my dad, a carpenter, could caress the grain in wood and just about make the wood sing. What would he think of his son's courting self-pity?

As the mist shifted, the Gospel Hump Mountains came into view. I loved how the clouds seemed to rub their pearly gray peaks into another season. What happened next is hard to explain exactly. I looked up and saw the cougar. He stood in the mist curled around us, close enough to touch, not moving. We looked at each other. Over his shoulder, I could see Gospel Peak covered with snow. Part of me wanted nothing more than to lie in the snow on the peak, slowly move my arms and make a great angel. I also wanted my father to be alive again and see this magnificence with me — we wouldn't have to say anything. I just wanted to hold his hand.

I was quite afraid — even to blink — but also calm. I wanted to see my father shake his head in wonder, the way he did after finishing a tough job, when he had to admit he was happy. Because if I moved, surely my heart would escape and fly off.

How long the cougar stayed I don't know. I remember how clear everything was — the pointy buds on my plum trees, his eyes, the dark whorls the knots made in the boards of my fence. And that perfect, priceless silence in his wake when he turned and went back, as smoothly it seemed as a trout in water.

Years have passed. I have not seen him — or any kills — so close again. Charley smiled when I told him about our meeting. "Maybe he figured this is your hunting ground."

Once upon a time, a big lion suddenly showed up and might have hurt me, or worse, but instead left me with a sharpened way of looking. I can see great distances — rain falling in fat columns miles away while the sun warms my bare shoulders. I can hear great distances too. A pine cone dropping branch by branch — *pwak! pwak!* Or the sudden flutter of a chukar's wings. When the two senses come together, it's often stunning. Moonlit nights, standing at my window, I can see a passage of the South Fork's curled brilliance that sounds like a woman removing and collecting in her hand a long string of favored pearls.

SANCTUARY

Utah — An expedition on the Green River leads this biologist and explorer through the heart of red rock cougar country, revealing the ecological subtleties of canyons and plateaus that the golden cats roam.

The tawny cougar seems born of rock, this rock in this canyon. . . . One easily imagines a cougar on a ledge above the river . . . a creature indistinguishable from the canyon, too distant to reveal the story of summer on the river, reflected back to us in its green-gold eyes.

—ELLEN MELOY, *RAVEN'S EXILE*

Rising abruptly from the floor of the San Rafael Desert are the Book Cliffs, named for the dark red striations horizontally running through the formation. When the sun is at low angles, the cliffs convey an image of a giant book resting on its side. From the south, the lower cliffs form an impenetrable wall of rock resembling a fortress capped with sandstone turrets.

These cliffs are but one of several prominent layers within a larger geologic structure called the Tavaputs Plateau. Collectively, these layers form an arc between the Wasatch Mountains of Utah and the Grand Mesa of Colorado, acting as a biogeographic corridor—an uninterrupted expanse of montane and subalpine plant communities ecologically connecting the Great Basin to the Rocky Mountains. The corridor helps to maintain demographic and genetic connectivity between populations of mesic-adapted species in an otherwise contiguous desert. Resembling a two-legged table, it is not a mountain range per se but more of a tilted escarpment;

the skeletal remains of a wetter time now oddly juxtaposed on a dry continent. Small gullies, hardly noticeable at first, quickly turn into major canyons, and flat plains narrow to ridges that dead-end four thousand feet above the desert floor. It is this pattern of beginning at the top and working down that characterizes sandstone country. Here, erosion is constant but, like the shape of the land, tends to be punctuated rather than continuous. Erosion is to the landscape as peer review is to the scientific method: a process that results in longevity not through an eruptive force but by whittling away the alternatives that do not hold up to scrutiny or time.

In between the starry-eyed town of Sedona and the 13,000-foot crest of the Uinta Mountains lies the Colorado Plateau — one of the most rugged and least accessible landscapes left in western North America. The Tavaputs are the central feature within this province. These sedimentary strata formed when the entire region was beneath an ancient sea. Over millions of years the basin was squeezed upward along massive fault lines, leaving it high and dry. Now the bottom is on top. It is these rocks and their distinct way of breaking down that give the area its character and moniker, Castle Country. No other part of the region so aptly exemplifies this description or its connotation.

AN OASIS IN THE DESERT

Cleaving the Tavaputs into two unequal parts is the Green River — the only passage through the Book Cliffs. The Utes referred to the river as Seedskeedee-Agee, meaning "prairie hen." The Spaniards, perhaps finding the native term cumbersome, named it Rio de los Ciboles (Bison River), and later changed it to El Rio Verde. The latter name resulted in the anglicized Green River, abbreviated even further in the vernacular to simply "the Green."

Independent of semantics, the river is the lifeblood of the desert. From its glacier-derived headwaters in Wyoming's Wind River Range, it is a meandering oasis in an otherwise parched landscape. The river winds down through the red rocks to its confluence with the Colorado River, where, like a bride, it gives up its name to the equally impressive but not necessarily larger stream.

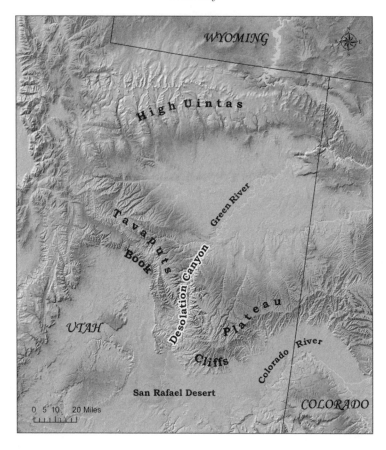

Water is a precious resource in the West and, paradoxically, is often most abundant in the driest of places. In 1964 the Green was impounded at Flaming Gorge, impacting a host of rare aquatic and riparian organisms that evolved under the warm, flashy flow of a shallow desert stream. The dam has reduced the frequency and intensity of spring flood events, and along with it the volume of sediment moving through the system. In turn, many ecological processes have been altered, from plant communities to spawning habitat for native fish.

The course of the Green is not just remote in spatial terms but temporally as well. In his journals, George Bradley, a crew member

on Powell's first voyage down the Green, lamented the inhospita-
bility of the area: "A terrible gale of hot, dry wind swept our camp
and roared through the cañon mingling its sound with the hollow
roar of the cataract making music fit for the infernal regions. We
needed only a few flashes of lightning to meet Milton's most vivid
conceptions of Hell." The Powell expedition named the canyon
Desolation.

I have come to this place with a crew conducting research on
the Green River fish community. Native species are declining in
the face of society's unyielding one-two punch: radically altered
habitat conditions compounded by competition with exotic game
fish. Ameliorating the combined effects of direct killing and habitat
loss is a common theme in modern practice of conservation biology. Along those lines, my interest in the canyon was its function
as a refuge for mountain lions. I had been involved with research
examining the spatial patterns of cougar mortality and wanted to
explore small pockets of remote habitat where cougars were not
likely to encounter people. The conclusions of my work were based
on the premise that hunting can have notable effects on cougar
society. Extrapolating, perhaps localities with little or no hunting
pressure might act as reservoir populations capable of supple-
menting outlying areas where cougars were more susceptible to
negative encounters with society. Coming here I had three primary
objectives: (1) determine if the area was indeed suitable habitat;
(2) search for evidence of cougar presence within the canyon corridor; and (3) if cougars were present, assess the reasons for the lack
of hunting pressure in the area. Desolation Canyon lies at the broken heart of a watershed covering more than one thousand square
miles, which, according to crude measures, provides suitable habitat with little human intrusion.

The fact that cougars are still as widespread as they are is a tes-
tament to their tenacity. More importantly, it is also a direct result
of their preference for rugged terrain. This animal exemplifies all
the qualities of a species vulnerable to extinction — large territories,
low densities, and conservative reproductive rates. Increasing road
densities make the cats' habitat more accessible, and the demand

for hunting opportunities continues to rise. Further hindering conservation efforts, this creature—often called "ghost cat"—is a virtual apparition and the ability to census it in a reliable and economical fashion remains elusive. In a shrinking world, their population status is in question.

Life flourishes along the river. Once on the water, solitude reigns. Moving water and birdsong are the only sounds. Most of the larger plants in this system, such as willow, maple, and cottonwood, occur in a thin band along the banks of the river. Away from the water the vegetation quickly transitions to sagebrush and other drought-adapted species. Where there is enough soil and moisture, shrubland gives way to piñon-juniper forest, and on the highest ridges Douglas fir and ponderosa pine can be seen spilling down the north-facing slopes.

As the boat drifts downstream it becomes apparent that the plant community is in a state of transition. An invader from the Mediterranean called tamarisk—or salt cedar—is out-competing other water-loving species that grow along the shoreline. Tamarisk was introduced to the Southwest as a shelter-belt tree during the nineteenth century and has now spread through most of the major watercourses in the region. Functionally, it reduces the inherent variability in the environment by stabilizing the banks, narrowing the channel, and sequestering groundwater. Ecologically, it tends to support lower biodiversity than the flood-adapted willows it is replacing. This tree also affects the dynamics of beach erosion and sandbar development, which, in conjunction with the dam, has led to declines in spawning habitat for the endangered Colorado pike minnow. Yet other species, such as the willow flycatcher, have adapted well to the replacement of native willows with tamarisk. Either way, over much of the Desert Southwest this plant now forms the dominant habitat type for species that depend on streamside forests.

PAINTED PONIES

The first night's camp was located on a broad sandbar on an inside meander. The moist sand was evidence that the water level was dropping quickly and that only a week or so prior this beach had been submerged. All day the weather had been threatening, but as darkness approached, it became clear that what had appeared to be an afternoon thunderstorm was settling in for the evening. In preparation, we staked down our tents and lashed the bowlines of the boats to a dead tree stranded at the high-water mark. With the waning of the day, the wind picked up, blowing sand across the beach in swirling patterns, helping me appreciate the sentiments of Powell's crew. The bank opposite our camp was a steep concave wall of sandstone capped by spires and hoodoos that silhouetted the southern horizon. As the storm intensified, lightning appeared sporadically as a broad arc above the ridge, illuminating the entire canyon for a split second at a time. Each thunderclap sounded like a cannon echoing through an amphitheater. It was following the first squall that I heard a foreign sound. It was the neighing of horses coming from the tributary behind camp. I could feel their hoof beats reverberate through the sand as they sought safe haven from the electricity.

Nevada and Wyoming have more wild horses than any other states, but wild horses are also common in Utah. Mustangs are found throughout the Book Cliffs, where they make up part of a larger population that spills into Colorado. Although *Equus* evolved in North America, all members of the genus became extinct here approximately eight thousand years ago. Today, horses found in the New World are feral animals of Eurasian origin. Accidentally or otherwise, they were reintroduced to Mexico by Spanish explorers during the 1600s. These herds expanded northward on their own, and over time their numbers were subsidized by animals that escaped from prospectors and pilgrims settling the western territories. *Equus caballus* is now firmly established across much of the western hemisphere. Native grasses and shrubs in this arid land have evolved for several millennia without grazing by horses. This repatriation may have come with some as yet poorly understood ecological implications for desert plant communities.

There are places in the deserts of western North America where wild horses have been identified as a staple grain for mountain lions. Indeed, one study conducted on Montgomery Pass in California's White Mountains found that foals constituted a significant proportion of the cougar diet during summer and fall. Predation was most pronounced in the higher elevations where steep terrain and piñon-juniper forests provided sufficient cover. Cougars preyed on the annual cohort into autumn, when either seasonal movements made their acquisition more difficult or the foals had matured to a size and savvy where they were no longer vulnerable. It is not clear whether lions would be there without the horses, or if the horses are relieving some of the predation pressure that might otherwise be directed at native ungulates such as deer and bighorn sheep. Nevertheless, under those conditions the native predator was able to incorporate the now exotic herbivore into its dietary repertoire.

The most fundamental component of habitat for any creature is the abundance and diversity of food resources. Regarding the mountain lion, habitat has one other primary component: the cover that enables it to acquire the food. The horse is a grazer, meaning that its diet is made up primarily of grasses and forbs, whereas deer are browsers, as their typical diet comprises shrubs. There is some evidence indicating that grazers may actually improve habitat for browsers, as they tend to preferentially impact plants that compete with shrubs for moisture and soil nutrients. In many shrub-steppe ecosystems, minimal dietary overlap may allow the coexistence of these large herbivores. In this country, horses are relegated to a landscape that is very amenable to the way a cat conducts its business. Broken terrain forces animals to use predictable routes to the water's edge, where dense vegetation provides ample stalking cover. The presence of horses may benefit the cougar both directly as a food resource and indirectly as a modifier of habitat for its preferred prey species, mule deer.

RAGGED EDGES

My duty as a member of this fleet is to pilot the supply boat. It is a large inflatable raft piled high with camping gear, scientific equipment, and other sundry "necessities." The canyon is nearly one hundred miles long, and numerous rapids punctuate an otherwise gentle current. The vegetation lining the banks is raucous with bird activity. At regular intervals great blue herons flush from backwater eddies where they hunt for small fish. The conditions for tracking here are beyond compare and I have plenty of time to drift into back bays and explore beaches for animal sign. It is August and the peak runoff has long passed with lingering patches of snow relegated to a few north-facing cirques in the higher reaches of the watershed. The farmers on either end of the canyon are drawing water from the river to irrigate their crops. We watch the water level drop with each passing day, as evidenced by the fine layer of silt left on the shore. It is this muddy canvas that provides a time stamp of the passing of creatures ranging in size from caterpillars to feral cattle. It is amazing how many species make a living within this narrow band of riparian woodland. On one beach I find sign of a black bear sow traveling with two cubs. As the trip proceeds I find evidence of horses at nearly every cottonwood spring or tributary.

Driftwood is everywhere. From its headwaters in northern Colorado to its confluence with the Green in Dinosaur National Park, the Yampa River is the largest tributary to the Green and a relic of the old regime. Combined with pulses from summer thunderstorms, the Yampa is responsible for a large amount of the untamed energy pulsing through Desolation Canyon. As a result, logs thirty feet long and a foot in diameter are stacked on rocks twelve feet above the current water level. Logjams and debris piles create habitat for insects, birds, and small mammals and building materials for beavers, while slowing the flow of sediment through the system. The Yampa remains a truly wild river, but its days as such may be numbered—four of the most rapidly growing states in the United States are in the Desert Southwest, where water is a commodity often spoken of in terms similar to those of oil and gold.

In the desert, water is the first and last limiting resource. In mountainous country, abrupt elevation gradients force hot air to rise and cool, thereby creating thunderstorms during the summer months. The plateau is made of sandstone, and water readily dissolves the bonds holding sand particles together. Moving water incises more rapidly in the vertical plane than in the horizontal, giving the land an inordinately steep character. The stairstep fashion in which sandstone erodes is evident on every scale, from the silt layers deposited on the beach, to the monolithic blocks that form the rim and widen the canyon at infrequent but noteworthy intervals. Flash flooding sends house-sized boulders cascading into the river, creating rock gardens and turbulence. Irregular gradients in the river contribute to the formation of rapids. Each is preceded and followed by languid water where sediment accumulates, creating backwaters and beaches that support localized gallery forests. The importance of these oases for wildlife is far greater than the total area they occupy. Cottonwood springs not only harbor resident animals but also act as transitional habitat for birds migrating between Mexico and the far northern latitudes.

NAGACHI AND TUKU—THE SHEEP AND THE BIG CAT

Three days into the trip I found what I was looking for. Numerous islands dot the river. Some are nothing more than ephemeral sandbars, whereas others have been stabilized by tamarisk and are now longer-term features of the river. It was on one of these islands that I detected conclusive evidence of cougar presence in the canyon.

One of my fellow crew members decided to explore the lee side of a moderate-sized island. Although these boats do not draw much water, they do require some, and this left our mate high and dry. I paddled in on the downstream side of the island where I could hike up the shore to help him out of the shallows. The water had recently receded and the mud in the channel was knee deep. Along its harder edge was an improvised trail. There in the drying mud was the track of a tom lion. Unmistakable in size and by the three-lobed heel, he had walked upstream along this backwater bank and vanished into the thickets. It was hard to tell how old the tracks were—several days at least. The blades of grass that had been pushed down under the weight of his foot had regained their posture. Additionally, small cracks were developing in the mud around the edges, indicating that the sun had baked the medium in which the event had been recorded. Serendipity has always played a significant yet unpredictable role not only in love but in scientific endeavors as well.

Potential prey species for the cougar were present, but elusive. It was in the deepest part of the canyon that I sighted several bighorn sheep on the cliffs above a major tributary. Seven sheep in all—four ewes, two lambs, and.a yearling ewe. They scrambled over the cliffs on the east side of the river. The Green did not appear to be much of a barrier to movement for wildlife, but it was interesting that most of the animals I had seen were on tribal lands, on the eastern side of the river.

The bighorn sheep is a creature with a tumultuous history—a quality unlikely to change in the future. Bighorn numbers dropped precipitously following the introduction of domestic sheep to western rangelands in the mid-nineteenth century. Diseases for which the native sheep had no immunity combined with market hunting left them extirpated from most of their historic range. Today, the bighorn represents a tenuous management success story. Symbolically reintroduced to many of its former haunts, it hangs on to a precarious future. Conservative reproductive rates, fire suppression, and competition with deer impede widespread recolonization. The halt in its decline is due largely to aggressive management driven by the desires and financial backing of trophy hunters eager for a chance to collect a specimen of this wilderness icon. Therein lies the rub. The bighorn inhabits some of the roughest and most remote country left in the West. Along with the golden eagle, the mountain lion is one of the few predators equally well-adapted to this terrain. Cougars have a proclivity for killing wild sheep, much to the chagrin of sportsmen's organizations. In less productive habitats, the generalist nature of this feline comes out, and its fondness for deer wanes in favor of whatever is readily available. The presence of bighorn indicates that there is yet another species that may in part sustain Big Whiskers.

It is quite clear why there are no cougars taken out of this drainage. Irrespective of habitat, there are few roads to gain access; the only way in or out is by boat, which during spring runoff is not a venture for the faint of heart and during winter all but the rapids are frozen. The land has only three prominent angles: flat, vertical, and the odd forty-five-degree slope that connects the two. Without trails or roads, even a mule would be hard-pressed to negotiate the steep, crumbling complexity that makes up this barren landscape.

The presence of humans and the importance of hunting are readily apparent in the rock art we find among the cottonwood springs. Petroglyphs are replete with references to animals. One panel illustrates a human figure pulling back a bow with an arrow pointed at something resembling a wild bighorn. Hunting has taken place here for a long time. It is quite possible that less hunting takes place in this canyon now than at any other time in the last millennia.

The descendents of these early hunters are still here, although relegated to precisely surveyed reservations on the eastern half of the Tavaputs Plateau. In the odd place where a trail or dirt road does reach the canyon bottom, there are prominent signs reminding travelers that from the river eastward are Ute tribal lands. The western side of the canyon is under the guidance of the Bureau of Land Management. Regardless of ownership, the Book Cliffs are part of a larger region rich in fossil fuels and, coincidentally, are not protected by wilderness designation. Portions of the canyon corridor have been eyed by energy companies eager to take advantage of the favorable political climate. Exploration is preceded by road development, which inevitably leads to greater access and subsequently the exploitation of all natural resources. When the stakes get high enough, even Eden becomes negotiable.

AUTUMN COLORS

In the wild nothing is sacred and change is the only constant. Humans do everything they can to maintain the status quo — whatever that may be. Such is every species. All organisms attempt to modify their immediate environment in such a way as to enhance the highs and minimize the lows. The quaking aspen is a common member of subalpine plant communities across North America. It is called mid-successional because it makes its living during the times following a major perturbation, such as an avalanche or fire. The things aspens cannot tolerate are aridity, shade, and an undisturbed environment. These factors, alone or in concert, presage the decline of aspens, and thus their absence from climax communities. Aspens also attempt to minimize variation in certain life-history requirements. Although they need frequent fires to kill off competitors, they also need predictable sources of water.

At the apex of Desolation Canyon, where its depth rivals that of the Grand, aspens cling on in the highest north-facing alcoves. During cooler and wetter times, the trees were much more widely distributed. As the climate warmed and dried, clones at lower elevations and on southerly aspects perished. Over time, aspens "retreated" to the refugia of the highest and wettest recesses of the mountain. The interesting thing about this phenomenon is that organisms do not necessarily move to better spots, so much as they die out at the edges of their range where changes in the environment are most apparent. Significantly, modern society has sought to eliminate wildfire, whereas pre-colonial inhabitants deliberately set fires because early successional plant communities supported more wild game. Historically, aspens were a direct beneficiary of early forest management and a lightning-rich climate.

In the Book Cliffs, the desiccating influence of the desert has pushed the tree with the fluttering leaves high into the last strongholds of its domain. In its wake come the drought-tolerant species, such as piñon pine, juniper, and, where fires have become scarce, Douglas fir—none of which can support the same abundance of wildlife as their predecessor. In the face of a drier climate and interference from man, the climax community arises and the competition continues between a different set of players, where again fire and water will arbitrate the outcome. Balance is only the average of extremes and exists, if at all, only for fleeting moments.

ALLEE AND EDGE EFFECTS: A SCIENTIFIC ASIDE

As once-contiguous species distributions develop holes, connectivity—or the unimpeded flow of individuals—decays. The result is an array of subpopulations of various sizes. Breaks can occur where mortality is too high or where habitat quality degrades and cannot support resident animals. Each subpopulation exhibits its own dynamics based on size and factors associated with reproduction and survival. Collectively, these subpopulations are referred to as a metapopulation, within which the relatively larger constituent populations become increasingly important for persistence. Some of the lateral connections and demographic redundancies built into the social structure of the species act to dampen the risk of extinction. For example, transients are young, sexually mature animals that wander within the population, waiting for the death of a resident and the availability of a territory. When this cohort disappears, reproduction may decline. This has been documented in southern California, where a lion population surrounded by the sprawl of Los Angeles lost its last resident male. Reproduction ceased for a year before a transient male finally finessed the gauntlet and entered the population.

In regions where cougar presence is becoming temporally spotty, Allee effects can occur. Named for W. C. Allee, a pioneering population ecologist during the 1930s and 1940s, this phenomenon occurs when animals become so scarce that breeding declines because potential mates are scattered too widely. This is the primary impediment to cougar recolonization of suitable habitat east of the Mississippi River. Transients dispersing eastward from the Rockies are present but are spread out over such a wide area that reproduction is untenable. Thus, Allee effects act to accelerate declines in a low-density population.

The edge effect is the geographic equivalent of a surface to volume ratio. A given subpopulation may be surrounded by unsuitable habitat, such that most home ranges abut or overlap some agent of mortality or impediment to movement. This in turn reduces or eliminates immigration, making population persistence wholly dependent upon internal reproduction. The more insidious effect is that of inbreeding and genetic isolation, which invariably follow in the wake of segregation. Such is the case of the Florida panther, and one of the primary reasons that population exhibits such a high conservation profile.

Because humans have exerted such a strong influence on ecological processes—via the introduction of exotic species, abbreviating successional pathways, and exploitation—the larger and presumably more demographically stable populations are likely to occur in areas less accessible to direct human interference. Current genetic evidence indicates that this may have already taken place with cougars on a large scale. The Pleistocene epoch was marked by extinctions or severe range contractions of a wide array of North American fauna. In conjunction with the fossil record, genetic studies suggest that cougars also may have been substantially reduced in distribution during that time. However, populations in the tropics—where the effects of climate change were less pronounced—buffered the species from extinction and acted as a source for the recolonization of North America following glacial retreat.

A CAT THE COLOR OF STONE

Even in a land far from civilization, biotic communities are anything but pristine. In the desert, species both loved and reviled by society interact. Some of the success stories of modern wildlife management are evident; counterbalancing these successes, however, are a host of aliens established through both negligence and premeditation. Fish in the river, plants along the banks, and feral livestock grazing the hills—all in an ecosystem altered by a now static river flow. The counterpoints to this consortium of ecological wild cards are the indigenous species that persist. Species with carnivorous tendencies have caused much consternation among human societies for occupying a niche with a high degree of overlap with our own. The large predators have been labeled as pests and therefore persecuted to the point that the wilder, more remote portions of their ranges represent their last chances for survival. The black bear and the mountain lion straddle a fine line—adaptable to human presence but vulnerable in the long run. The cougar is often invoked as a symbol of wilderness; yet, it is such only because that is how we perceive it in our common mythos and, more importantly, what we make it by our own hand. Semi-urban cougar populations illustrate that this species does not require pristine wilderness to survive. Nevertheless, the social hysteria and destruction of habitat surrounding non-wilderness cougars clearly demonstrate the motives and means by which humans relegate their demons to the hinterlands.

In wilderness these creatures occur despite the tempest outside. Their once expansive and continuous ranges have been fractured, not forcing them into remote areas but making their welcome anywhere else so lukewarm that it is only in the wild areas that they persist. Where the desert gnaws away at the garden, a new community is forming. One in which vestiges of the old world either make do or make way for competitors spilling over the battlements. This begs the question, is the cougar a member of the old guard vainly holding together a crumbling ecosystem or the ultimate opportunist thriving on an ecosystem in flux? The erosion of one species' distribution may coincide with the invasion and spread of a new one. New members filling niches of extinct natives or, like the cougar, old ones maintaining a role they have always played — but interacting with a different cast of characters. New ecosystems arise.

The lion of the mountains still roams this sandstone citadel. On the far end of the canyon the cliffs diminish in stature and the river widens as it flows into the San Rafael. An old tire lies stranded on a sandbar where the Price River drains into the Green. In the evening, the pungent scent of burning sage and piñon pine rises up through the air. The day wanes as I listen to the breeze blowing through the cottonwood leaves overlaid on the rhythm of moving water. The low-angle sun illuminates colors within the rocks that are all but invisible during the heat of the day. The west-facing wall of the canyon is lit up in a bright red, as though a light were coming from within the stone. A great blue heron soars above the river on an invisible current of air in time with the turbulence of the water. And, somewhere, a whisker twitches.

J U L I A   B .   C O R B E T T

TALKING WITH A COUGAR

Utah – A seemingly benign visit with a cougar calls on this author to revisit her communication with all animals.

Anyone with a pet knows that hint of movement out of the corner-most reaches of your vision that tells you of the presence of another. That's how I first see her, a whisper of movement without sound, a sense before a confirmation. A cougar.

It's a simultaneous glance, me turning left, her turning right. Fifteen feet away, maybe twenty. Tail, god, so much tail. Thick, lush, the color of cooled butterscotch. *Puma concolor*, the cat of one color. Except she isn't. A darker stripe, beginning at her rump, travels down the top of her tail and ends in a dark chocolaty tip. Her belly and chest are butterscotch with milk stirred in. Her body angles away, head turned back toward me. I hold my breath, hold my body mid-motion, freezing the moment to study like a painting.

Between us are a few sagebrush and scrub oak bushes; behind me is a cliff of golden sandstone that I just left. She was studying me when I was out there, I know she was. A human, so quiet, so motionless, legs crossed, fingers upturned and slightly curled, hands resting on the knees. My mind out there on that rock, however, was anything but still. The thoughts rushed in. The noise in my truck's rear axle. Data analysis. My recently failed romance. The usual. When I meditate, I try to acknowledge the thoughts as they pop up and then let them pass through, like the ticker tape that runs across the bottom of the TV screen announcing severe weather or basketball scores. Eventually the thoughts slowed, my shoulders sagged, and the tightness around my eyes slackened. My breathing softened and deepened, and the patient, steady wind over the cliff edge became white noise. A sudden slap of wind and gathering darkness on the backs of my eyes is what prompted me to open them and clamber off the cliff and into the woods, face to face with the cougar.

"Wow."

I don't realize the word has left my lips until I hear it. I can't believe I'm standing in front of a cougar. Or a mountain lion, puma, panther, all names for the second largest feline in the western hemisphere. Creature of snarls and ferocity in old Westerns, frequently debased to advertising cars and football teams, but revered by native peoples for its connection to God. The wild one before me, one of the most secretive large mammals of the West, can't be one and the same.

I am planning on this encounter lasting just seconds, which was the length of my only other cougar encounter nearly fifteen years before in Idaho's White Cloud Mountains. That time, I was squatting outside the tent at 5:00 A.M., first-light in midsummer, when a cougar materialized on the slope opposite me; by the time I blinked and pushed up my glasses, the apparition—consisting mostly of tail—had vanished. There's no way this one will stay, no way; this is fleeting, ethereal.

"You are so beautiful," I whisper.

She stares and begins to flick the dark tip of her tail, first left, then right, and back again. I stare, right into her eyes. I don't remember that with some animals—wolves, maybe bears too, I can't remember—you're not supposed to look them in the eye but to avert your gaze and play submissive. I'm not sure about big cats, but it's too late anyway. I inch a hand down into the camera case hanging around my neck. There are a few glimmers in my head, none of them lasting long enough to register, of recommended actions when you meet a cougar. Picture-taking isn't one of them, but this is a meeting I want recorded.

I haven't taken many pictures this trip because of the "male rains," the name the Navajo give the late-summer, early-fall monsoons because of their intensity and violence. A cloudburst of male rain on a mesa can fill a slot canyon fifteen miles away with a charging mass of muddy water twelve feet high. For the two days since we arrived in the La Sal Mountains of southeastern Utah, rain has beat down on prickly pear and piñon pine, cutting gullies and washes through tight and tangled patches of brush.

During the downpours, Becky, Camille, and I read in our borrowed cabin, listening to the syncopated *thwack, whack, whop* of rain pellets on the green metal roof. In moments of clearing, we ventured out in rain pants and slickers, swishing along until sunlight steamed the rocks and we were forced to strip down. Back and forth, layering and stripping, turbulence and calm, wavering on the cusp of summer and fall.

"Were you watching me on that rock?" I whisper. "My god you are so gorgeous." I unzip the camera case.

Still fearing she'll vanish, I choose the automatic setting. *Zzzz, zhhmmm,* the noisy autofocus slides into position. Her tail like a silent metronome bobs left, bobs right. It isn't a spastic twitching like my cat does before he pounces but more like a marker that my presence, my conversation, is entirely noticed. The midafternoon sky hangs darkly; I pop up the auto-flash. Without leaving our mutual gaze, I slowly pull the camera up to my eyes and shoot. The auto advance—*zzzrr rrr rrieehh*—cracks as loudly as dry kindling.

No movement from the cougar, except the metered tail, despite being shot with a camera and flashed with light. I take another.

"Thank you. Thank you so much," I say, louder than a whisper now, but hushed. I feel ready to explode, maybe with tears, maybe with a giddy giggle.

She takes three steps to the side, turns, and sits, facing me. Regal, dramatically regal. She blinks her eyes, slow, deliberate blinks, blinks like the "I love you blinks" you get from your cat. Almost blissful. With domestic kitty behavior as a guide, she looks positively sleepy. The tail is quiet now, wrapped around her. I snap one more picture.

In this moment, neither of us is afraid. We share this. I know this more than I've ever known anything. Through the wisps of bare branchlets between us, the ether blends our marrow, our essence, our species. I am talking to a cougar and have never felt so powerful in all my life. Fire fills my flushed cheeks, yet on the inside, I'm blue, cool, and big. Very big. I'm utterly out there, alone and unguarded, yet entirely not alone. It is the most pure moment I have ever shared with another creature.

And that's what friends question about this story: "Wait a minute, weren't you afraid? My god, you were taking flash pictures of a large predator!"

"I know. But all I felt was powerful."

"And you were talking to it?"

Well, talking is a pretty anthropocentric way of looking at it. What a cat hears from "talking" — according to that *Far Side* cartoon — is a lot of blah blah blah. How human of us to think we have cornered the market on meaningful communication. Our words are crafted with design, strung together with intent and outcome in mind; they're never really very accurate, or at least very complete. There's no faking a sense, a presence without a protective package, as when you're around a horse you're afraid of. The horse knows. You move with fear, smell like fear, become it; the words "Whoa, nice horsey" are just "Blah, blah, blah."

My words to that cougar are conveying something, I have no doubt, but the words themselves matter not at all. Like a newborn not understanding its mother's speech, yet precisely and immediately tracking her emotions through touch and tone and posture and movement and mood, and then mirroring back; reciprocal, deep, undeniably — unintentionally — honest. Whatever I am expressing to that cougar, she is mirroring it back to me; we are partaking of each other.

I can't pinpoint when this divine communion begins to melt, when the power and peace evaporate. Maybe it was like a stare-down, and I just blinked first. It was a shift I didn't feel I even participated in. First, I noticed the rapid boom of my heart. And I thought, *This is so strange that she hasn't left. This is simply not normal. Not normal at all. How did she know I was on that rock meditating? Did she smell me on my moon, smell my menstrual blood? Is she sizing me up right now? And why on earth am I calling it a "she"?*

Most animals seem to have social distances with humans. Earlier in the day, an immature turkey vulture perched on a snag a hundred feet from the cabin was most expressive about his comfortable distance; he always flapped away with a labored *whoosh* of wings when I crossed the very same invisible yard line. But with this cougar, I am feeling no boundaries, as if I could snap flash pictures and talk all day and she'd just keep blinking. It is unnerving. If neither one of us is afraid, perhaps one of us ought to be. And perhaps that should be me.

This reasoning flashes through me in nanoseconds, but its effect on my presence, my being there with her, is irreparable. I need to end this encounter; I need to leave. I pick up a silver stick lying to the right of my feet and wave it over my head. They say with some animals you need to make yourself look larger.

Firmly and loudly now, I say, "Go on! Get out of here! Git!"

Slow, sleepy blinks from the cougar. She clearly is not finished with our moment.

I glance ahead to detect a path and begin putting one foot behind the other, almost walking sideways. Reluctant to turn my back on her, I take slow measured steps toward the cabin, which is at least a hundred yards down the ridgeline, carrying my stick. I try not to step on noisy things or make sudden movements, as if that actually matters. Twenty yards, I stop, turn. She pauses, mid-step, the distance between us unchanged. I hope this qualifies as a socially acceptable distance. Cougars can easily leap the distance that separates us now.

I don't know how to view her: inquisitive feline following me home or large predator sizing me up, considering which flank to bite first. She has given absolutely no clue of ferocity, more like curiosity, yet I'm uncomfortable being the object of it. The attention is too intense.

I stop, face her, and bang my stick against a tree, "Go on! Go away!" They say with bears you need to make noise. The stick shatters, desiccated by the high desert clime. I feel naked; she sees the vulnerable that's displaced the powerful, I know she does. Frenetically I pull on a clump of branches, but it's still rooted; only a small branchy piece gives way. I grab again, quickly check the cougar's location, grab and pull, tug, tug and strain. The desert earth, although softened by the rains, won't yield the weapon. I resume my retreat, wildly pushing aside branches that *whap* back at me. My rain pants make a colossal noise against the brush, and cactus pads stick in my boots.

"You guys!" I yell toward the cabin, where Becky and Camille stayed to dry off after our hike. I know they're still beyond earshot, but in this shrubby jumble I won't see the cabin until I'm upon it. Again I yell, "You guys!"

I pause, panting. I half expect the cougar to appear in front of me next, without warning. She trots without touching the ground. She is that quiet; I am that noisy. I try to check my panting, quiet my heart. I turn just my head. The cougar has paused, still behind me, the distance between us maintained as if by tape measure. Oh god. I'm not walking now, not running either, more like the in-between hurried gait that spurs teachers to call out, "Now walk, don't run!"

"Beckyyy!" I whine.

The cougar has not growled, showed teeth, stalked, or crouched in any way, but I'm not thinking these finer details. I'm running with, from, beside a cougar that three minutes ago I was talking to.

"Help!"

I trust the cougar is still behind me; I've quit turning around.

"What is it?" I hear from the direction of the cabin.

"There's . . . a cougar . . . chasing me," I get out between gasps.

A long pause, then, "You're joking, right?"

The cabin is in sight now. Becky comes down the front steps. "Oh my god, there she is." She doesn't mean me but the cougar, who has stopped about twenty-five feet away, half tucked under the sloping lower branches of a piñon. When Camille appears, the cougar evaporates, I don't even know which direction.

That evening, Becky and Camille applaud my chutzpah and bravery. I bask in cougar glow. I got to talk with a cougar. I made her blink, slowly. The fearful feelings fade behind the powerful ones, but my heart pounds through my ears when I go alone to the pit toilet before bed.

I know that I attract animals, or that somehow they are attracted to me. More times than I can count, people are amazed how their timid dog or skittish cat immediately comes to me. Friends say they always see more animals and birds when hiking with me, but I attributed that to above-average powers of observation. I guess I always have talked to animals, as strange as that may sound. Squeak to pikas, caw to ravens, call out barred owls, and I even conversed with an elk once. It's an honor when they talk back or move closer. But I always assumed the talking was strictly for my enjoyment, not theirs. I shouldn't have doubted that some sort of connection might be taking place; Chief Dan George said that if you talk to the animals, they will talk with you, and you will know each other.

She still appears in my life, this cougar, as well she should. I sometimes see her face against a shimmering violet background in that space behind my eyes when I meditate. I framed one of the pictures I took of her and hung it over my bed. I've checked out library books on cougars and asked biologists what her actions meant. I learned that her behavior may have indicated well-meaning to a strange creature assumed to be a peer, which allowed her to stay with me, follow me, and be curious about this woman taking pictures. If my presence had communicated either fear or threat, she might have perceived me as potential prey, or she wouldn't have shown herself at all. Tail flicking was her sign of agitation or alertness, which ceased when she felt more comfortable with me. Her slow blink, blink, blink was her way of watching intently, focusing on and trying to figure out this creature talking to her — a more submissive way of processing information without making direct eye contact. But sadly, most of what I've learned about cougars from newspaper stories is how to be afraid and to avoid moments with cougars. Those stories said I was supposed to avoid eye contact and not hike alone.

An encounter such as mine can be interpreted many ways, but regardless, I know that it meant something, that it signaled something. In the religious lexicon of my youth, this cougar was an epistle, delivering a message of transformation. The Chickasaw even called the cougar the "cat of God." To Native Americans, bushmen, and others who recognize humanity as a part of nature, cougar was my totem animal, carrying a message of personal power — about testing power and learning to use it.

And what is power but a complex amalgamation of force and fear, strength and submission, advance and retreat, like inseparable twins, appearing simultaneously in situations — and with creatures — outside ourselves? Not unlike talking with a cougar one moment and running from it the next.

S T E V E   P A V L I K

THE SACRED CAT
THE ROLE OF THE MOUNTAIN LION IN
NAVAJO MYTHOLOGY AND TRADITIONAL LIFEWAY

*Arizona – The practice of traditional Navajo ways is waning and,
with it, the knowledge of the honored role of the puma in hunting,
ceremony, and daily life.*

The Navajos are the largest tribe of
American Indians in the United States. Numbering over 200,000
in population, they inhabit a 27,000-square-mile reservation in the
Four Corners region of the American Southwest, mostly in Arizona
with the remainder in northwestern New Mexico and a small section of southeastern Utah.

The land of the Navajos is extremely diverse in its physical
makeup. Most of the geography is sparse desert country, Great
Basin desert shrub, grasslands accented by red rock sandstone
canyons and often spectacular rock formations. Scattered throughout the desert landscape are mountains, petran montane (Rocky
Mountain) and subalpine conifer forests thick with piñon, juniper,
and pine. Elevations in the mountainous regions can exceed nine
thousand feet. This diversity lends itself to an equally diverse vari-
ety and abundance of wildlife. Among the wild inhabitants of the
Navajo reservation is the mountain lion, *Puma concolor.* The Navajo

name for the mountain lion is *nashduitso*—a word that generally reflects the hunting nature of this animal. Most Navajos, however, simply use the common western name, cougar.

In modern times perhaps only about 5 percent of the Navajo people can be classified as being what I have termed "orthodox Navajo"—individuals who continue to follow the way of life pre-scribed to them by their deities, a compilation of supernatural beings called the Holy People. Most contemporary Navajos follow other spiritual paths, most notably the Native American Church (NAC) and various forms of Christianity. Still, many Navajos attempt to incorporate elements of traditionalism into their daily lives. Increasingly, young Navajos are seeking to relate to the natu-ral world in a traditional way.

Unfortunately, much traditional knowledge has been forgot-ten and can only be found in earlier, hard-to-find anthropological publications. I hope that this piece of writing makes something of a contribution to Navajo people in bringing together a small part of the anthropological literature on the mountain lion, and offers to non-Navajo people an alternative way of looking at and thinking about this species.

NAVAJO MYTHOLOGY AND RELIGION

The people we now know as the Navajos are a product of a coming together of two very different cultures, the Southern Athabaskans, or Apacheans, and the Pueblos. The Southern Athabaskans arrived in the American Southwest in a number of separate bands at dif-ferent times, by different routes, and settled in different locations. In general, they diverged to become two different groups that more or less shared a common language: the Apaches—who fur-ther divided into various eastern and western subgroups—and the future Navajos. The date of the Southern Athabaskan arrival into the Four Corners area is unclear but probably occurred in the early 1500s. The exact location of this arrival and early settle-ment was the upper San Juan River valley of southwestern New Mexico and, specifically, Blanco, Largo, Carrizo, and Gobernador Canyons and their surrounding drainages. Traditional Navajos know this area today as Dinetah and consider it to be their Holy Land.

The Southern Athabaskans lived in the Dinetah region for approximately two hundred years in relative isolation. During this time, they came in contact with a number of other native cultures, most notably the Pueblo tribes of the Rio Grande to the south. Often they raided these Pueblos but traded with them as well. In all probability, Southern Athabaskan culture remained relatively unchanged during this period. They were primarily hunters and gatherers with strong religious and other cultural traditions centering on the practice of hunting game. In time, however, these Athabaskans began to slowly acquire more of an agricultural and pastoral lifestyle from the Pueblos. This included raising sheep and goats initially brought into the Southwest by the Spanish.

In 1680 the Pueblos launched a great revolt against the Spanish and drove the repressive Europeans out of the Rio Grande Valley. Eventually the Spanish reclaimed the area by conquest in 1694. In the interim, hundreds, perhaps thousands, of Pueblos sought refuge from Spanish reprisal among their more warlike Southern Athabaskan neighbors to the north. The resulting amalgamation of these two distinct people with distinct ways of life provided the genesis for the tribe we today know as the Navajos.

The Navajo people have retained their Athabaskan language and with it a primarily Athabaskan identity. In most other ways, however, the syncretism leaned heavily toward the co-roots of their Pueblo heritage. From the Pueblos the Navajo acquired agriculture and livestock, the art of weaving and perhaps silversmithing, and the addition of several clans or families. But nowhere is the cultural debt more prevalent than in the area of mythology, religion, and ceremonial practices. Although the Navajos clung to some elements of the early Athabaskan religion, including that which anthropologist Karl W. Luckert calls the "Navajo Hunter Tradition," much that we now consider as being "traditional" Navajo is actually derived from Pueblo beliefs and practices. This is especially true in regard to the creation, or origin, stories that Navajos have handed down to their children through oral tradition for hundreds of years. In addition, many specific aspects of Navajo ceremonialism are of Pueblo origin, including the belief in certain deities and the use of masked dancers, sandpaintings, prayer sticks, and corn pollen in their religious ceremonies.

The Navajo creation stories form the foundation for Navajo traditionalism. These stories chronicle the mythological journey of the Navajo people through four underground worlds into the fifth, or current, world and to the beginnings of recorded history. These stories are the sacred history of the Navajo people. Moreover, they provide a blueprint for tribal life. They tell the Navajo people who they are, what their place in the world order is, and, most importantly here, how to conduct their personal relationships with the Earth and all other living things.

The Navajo creation stories, as noted earlier, also deal with the Navajo emergence through the underworlds into the present world where they currently live. Throughout these stories the Navajos, beginning with First Man and First Woman, interact with other beings, including their deities, the Holy People. Among the more important of these supernatural holy beings are Sun, Talking God, Calling God, Black God, and the beloved Changing Woman and her two twin hero sons, Monster Slayer and Child Born of Water. The underworlds are also home to a host of Animal People, who are generally envisioned as anthropomorphic beings. They exist as equals to the deities and humans, possess supernatural power, have the ability to communicate with both gods and mankind, and eventually migrate to the Fifth World as well. Some scholars consider the Animal People to be deities, or at least near-deities, superior to mankind in terms of the power they possess. Over time, these Animal People would lose most of their anthropomorphic qualities to assume the forms and roles they now possess. Thus, Mountain Lion became the mountain lion that still inhabits the more remote mountainous regions of the Navajo reservation today. Significantly, traditional Navajos believe that the Animal People did not lose all of their supernatural powers. Bears, for example, are considered to be the most powerful of the Animal People and still retain their ability to transform into other shapes and forms, including that of human beings. Most animals are also believed to possess the ability to transmit sickness to any human who commits a transgression against them. Thus, traditional Navajos define various categories of illness, such as "bear sickness," "coyote sickness," and "deer sickness." The origins of these illnesses, and the means to cure them, are found in the Navajo creation stories.

Sickness, disease, and injuries are treated in traditional ceremonies called "sings." Generally, these ceremonies are named after some element of the creation story associated with them. Bear sickness, for example, is cured through a ceremony known as the Mountainway ceremony, because the story associated with this sickness occurred in the mountains and mountains remain the home of bears. Other ceremonies include Enemyway, Shootingway, Beautyway, Nightway, Beadway, and Windway. Many of these ceremonies last nine days and nights and cost the host families thousands of dollars to organize. Leland C. Wyman and Clyde Kluckhohn, in their definitive classification of Navajo ceremonies, list fifty-eight distinct rituals not counting the various Huntingway ceremonies. Of these, only nine are considered extinct.

A Navajo who is in need of care for illness or injury will first consult a diagnostician who, through divine ability, will be able to determine the cause of the problem. The inflicted person will next seek out the services of a specialist who is trained to cure his or her problem. These specialists are known as "singers" or, more commonly to outsiders, as medicine men. In administering to his patient, the singer will conduct a ceremony in which he — most singers are men — will re-create through song and prayer the mythological events that explain the illness. He will also employ a number of other techniques and activities that might include giving medicine and utilizing sandpaintings — intricate pictorial representations drawn with colored sand — of the Holy People and other sacred images. The main purpose of the sandpaintings is to attract the Holy People so that they can use their powers to assist in the act of curing the patient. Major ceremonies are usually conducted inside a traditional Navajo structure called a hogan. The final nights of some ceremonies, such as the Mountainway, Shootingway,

Beautyway, and Nightway, are public events in which teams of masked dancers called *yeibichais* perform. Hundreds of spectators may attend this final performance.

Most Navajos today are not strictly traditional. The majority of Navajos — perhaps as many as 75 percent — belong to the Native American Church. The NAC is a pan-Indian religion that incorporates a generic Native American philosophy with elements of traditional religion and Christianity. It is characterized by the use of the psychedelic cactus peyote. The NAC was established on the Navajo reservation in the early 1930s, but it was only after World War II that the religion began to grow in popularity. As NAC membership has grown, traditionalism has declined. Along the way traditional knowledge has also been lost, as well as much of the understanding and respect for the natural world that for so long characterized the Navajo relationship with the land and its wild inhabitants.

NAVAJO MYTHOLOGY AND THE MOUNTAIN LION

Mountain lions have long played an important role in the Native American experience. One group of Native people to whom cougars seemed especially important was the prehistoric Anasazi Indians (A.D. 217–1299) who were the ancestors of the Pueblos — and thus indirectly ancestors to the Navajos. This close relationship is perhaps best illustrated by the many rock art images of mountain lions that were left behind by the Anasazi after these relics of art were discovered centuries later. Frequently the Anasazi depicted the mountain lion ritualistically, often wearing ceremonial items such as feathers, rainbows, and shamanistic hats. The image of the mountain lion as an anthropomorphic being, perhaps as a deity possessing supernatural power, reached its highest measure of expression along the Pecos River in Texas at a site named Panther Cave. Historic Pueblos possess a particularly rich body of mythological beliefs regarding mountain lions. In all probability it was through the Pueblos that the Navajos acquired much of their own cougar mythology.

In the Navajo creation story, Mountain Lion first appears in the Second World, also known as the Blue World. Numerous other

Cat People also inhabit this world, including Wild Cat (undoubtedly the first bobcat) and Spotted Lion, a being anthropologist Gladys A. Reichard identifies as a jaguar. In the Upward Moving and Emergence Way myth, as recorded by Father Berard Haile, Mountain Lion is singled out by Changing Woman and assigned to be one of the special "pets" to the Navajo people and, specifically, to one of the four original clans, the Kiyaa'aanii, or "Towering House People." In this story the four clans embark on a journey in which they are attacked by an enemy whom Haile identifies as Ute Indians. During the attack one of the men pleads to Mountain Lion, "My pet, we are sorely pressed, will you not help us?" In describing what transpired next, Father Berard Haile writes: "In a bound Mountain Lion was through the smoke hole, swept around the enemy, and tore them to pieces or bit off their arms as he circled them four times. After that he returned to his former place without a word."

Following this incident, Mountain Lion and the other pets — Bear, Big Snake, and Porcupine — who also helped fight off the Utes, presumably because they had now tasted human blood, had become so mean that they were dismissed by the clans into the mountains where they now preside in their present forms. Because of the service Mountain Lion rendered to the people, certain clans will not harm cougars, and traditional members of the Kiyaa'aanii clan continue to keep mountain lion pelts for the protective power they are believed to possess. The special relationship that exists between the Kiyaa'aanii clan and mountain lions provides a background to many other beliefs that Navajos have about cougars. It is also probably no accident that the Kiyaa'aanii clan traces its origins to an outlier settlement of the prehistoric Anasazi stronghold of Chaco Canyon. Polly Schaafsma notes that mountain lions are a particularly common rock art motif throughout the Chaco Canyon region.

Mountain Lion also appears as a protector in a number of other Navajo stories, including that of the Blessingway ceremony. In this story the hero twins — Monster Slayer and Child Born of Water — undertake a journey in search of their father, the Sun. Upon reaching his house in the cosmos they find that Mountain Lion, along with Bear, Big Snake, Thunder, and Wind, serves as a guardian blocking their way. In order to gain entrance, the twins had to first speak Mountain Lion's "sacred" name, He Who Is Speckled Over With Earth. Upon doing so, Mountain Lion allows them to pass through the gates. When the twins enter the Sun's house they find his walls to be covered with the skins of mountain lions—a sign of the richness and power of their father. Because of this story, mountain lion skins are considered to be a sign of wealth even today among the Navajos. Such is the case in the Blessingway ceremony, a common ritual known to many traditional Navajos in which certain "wealth songs" are sung to ensure good fortune and prosperity. One song, known to only a few Navajos, includes a passage referring to the Sun's house being "covered from wall to wall with mountain lion skins." The father of my principal Navajo mentor knows this wealth song in its entirety and jealously guards its exact words. When he performs the Blessingway ceremony, he never uses this special song in the presence of anyone other than close family members.

The story of the twins' visit to the Sun ends with the powerful deity acknowledging that he is indeed their father. He then gives them the weapons and knowledge they will need to return to the Earth and battle the monsters that are plaguing the Navajo people. The elder brother—Monster Slayer—becomes the ultimate warrior who slays most of the monsters.

The tale of his exploits continues in the Enemyway story. One of the weapons given to Monster Slayer by his father is a special bow and set of arrows. The arrows are kept in a quiver made of mountain lion skin with the long tail left dangling from the end. Eventually Monster Slayer teaches the Navajo people how to make these quivers; the majority of quivers used later by Navajo warriors and hunters are made of cougar skin. Navajos also wore hunting or war caps made of the caped head skin of the mountain lion—another tradition that traces its origins to Monster Slayer in the creation stories. Presumably, by wearing the skin of the cougar and by keeping their arrows in a cougar-skin quiver, the Navajo hunter or warrior acquired the characteristics of the master feline—stealth, speed, power, and courage.

Mountain Lion also appears in the Beadway myth. In this story he is traveling to actually perform a Beadway ceremony for a patient when he encounters his close friend Wolf, who is on a similar mission. Since neither wants to miss the other's sing, they agree that Mountain Lion should postpone his for one night. To bind the agreement the two great hunters—who often appear together in Navajo mythology—exchange quivers. A sandpainting used in the Beadway ceremony marks this trade and shows Mountain Lion carrying Wolf's white quiver and Wolf carrying Mountain Lion's yellow quiver. Two images of Spotted Lion appear in this sandpainting as well. In another Beadway sandpainting, Mountain Lion, Wolf, and Spotted Lion are joined by fellow hunters Wildcat, Lynx, and Badger and are depicted in a dance formation. What is unusual about this sandpainting is that these great hunters are shown wearing packs of corn on their backs, an unusual agricultural reference to beings that are usually associated with hunting and war.

In the Eagle Way story, a myth closely related to that of Beadway, Monster Slayer encounters White Shell Girl and Turquoise Girl, both daughters of Changing Woman. He tells them of a location where they can find a deer killed by Mountain Lion. "If you go there," he tells them, "you can see what a deer looks like and even obtain a piece of skin." The girls locate the dead deer and cut off a piece of hide, which they later scrape and fashion into a sack to carry seed. This is the origin of "sacred buckskin," deerskin that is not perforated by the holes caused by an arrow or, in modern times, by a bullet. Sacred buckskin, or "unwounded" buckskin as it is also called, is believed to possess special power since it retains the life forces of the deer and thus is absolutely essential in the making of medicine bags, masks, and other ceremonial items.

In another Navajo story—this one associated with the Red Antway ceremony—Mountain Lion and Wolf are attacked by Lightning after they have killed a game animal belonging to that deity. Lightning begins his assault by shattering a tree under which the two hunters were butchering their kill. Angered, Mountain

Lion holds up a magical whisker toward the sky. He then sings and prays, and Lightning falls to the ground before him. Mountain Lion then blows away the black cloud of Lightning, thus allowing the Sun to shine through. "I thought I was the only destroyer," Lightning said to Mountain Lion, "but you are more powerful than I am." In honor of Mountain Lion, Lightning gives him a song and a prayer to the Ant People.

Many other mountain lion beliefs and practices are scattered throughout Navajo traditional culture, and most of them trace their origins directly or indirectly back to the creation stories. Several additional beliefs and practices deserve at least mention here.

Navajos—even most nontraditional tribal members—possess a strong belief in the existence and danger posed by ghosts and witches. In the Upward-Reaching Way ceremony, or Evil Way ceremony as it is more commonly known, singers wear bandoliers and wristlets decorated with mountain lion claws. This ritual is the fundamental ceremony employed specifically for the treatment or prevention of disease, illness, and misfortune caused by ghosts. Mountain lion claws are used because, as one early Navajo informant explained, "Ghosts are afraid of mountain lions." Mountain lions are also said to be the only power that is feared by witches.

Mountain lion skin is also used to make hair ties for girls during their puberty ceremony, the *kinaalda*. This ceremony is a reenactment of the first puberty ceremony that was held in the Navajo stories for Changing Woman. The type of skin used for the hair tie, either cougar, deer, mountain sheep, or otter, is determined by the personality the young girl has demonstrated while growing up, or the type of personality her family wants her to acquire. Mountain lion skin is used to tie the hair of a girl who appears to be tough, forceful, cunning, or athletic, a so-called tomboy. The tie itself is a strip of skin, two fingers wide and cut from the nose to the tail of the cat. These ties are highly prized and are handed down through the family. My friend Will Tsosie's grandmother, as the matriarch of her family, is the keeper of a six-foot-long mountain lion hair tie that has been used to the point of falling apart, has been repaired, and used again for generations. Most of the women in this family whom I have met certainly seem to possess the strong admirable traits of cougar.

Navajos also possess a large body of traditional hunting knowledge and ritual, much of it focusing on the mountain lion. Anthropologists trace this aspect of Navajo culture not so much to the Pueblo-inspired creation stories but rather to the earlier Athabaskan origins of the tribe. In an earlier prehuman time, Navajos believed there once existed a group of master, or divine, hunters—Mountain Lion, Spotted Lion, Wolf, and Wildcat among them—who had been taught how to hunt by the game animals themselves, most notably by the Deer People. In turn, these divine hunters, each in his own special way, later taught humans how to hunt. Consequently, there is a specific Mountain Lion Way of hunting, also called the "Tiptoe" way of hunting, so named because it emphasizes the stealthy stalking methods used by mountain lions when poignantly hunting deer. This hunt was highly ritualized and was conducted under the direction of a singer familiar with it. During the hunt the hunter became a mountain lion and acted accordingly. Mountain lion fetishes—images of a cougar carved from stone—were used to gain the power of the divine hunter, and special prayers and songs were offered. One of these songs included the following passage and reflects the intimate relationship that existed between the Navajo hunter, the game animal he sought, and the mountain lion whom he sought to emulate:

> He goes out hunting
> The Mountain lion I am
> With mahogany bow he goes out hunting
> With the yellow tail-feathered arrow he goes out hunting
> The finest of female game
> Through the shoulder that I may shoot
> In death it obeys me.

A special relationship has long existed between traditional Navajo lifeway and the mountain lion. Sadly, this is a relationship that is fading as traditional Navajo beliefs begin to disappear. As I noted at the start of this essay, few Navajos follow the traditional path.

In addition, only a handful of mountain lions continue to live in Navajo Country. The last official cougar to be killed on the reservation was taken in 1978. I have talked to ranchers and sheepherders who continue to graze their livestock in the beautiful Chuska and Lukachukai Mountains of the reservation and several have told me that they occasionally catch a glimpse of the great cat. I have also on occasion seen mountain lion tracks in these mountains. When Chris Boligano, for her excellent book *Mountain Lion: An Unnatural History of Pumas and People*, interviewed a Navajo Fish and Game official, who was also a tribal member, in the mid-1990s, Chris was told, "We know we have lions, but we don't know much about lion populations." The official then added, "I'd like to see a research project to determine whether we could have a sport hunting season which would bring income from licenses." White or Navajo, the bottom line always seems to be the almighty dollar.

At the present time the Navajo Nation does not have a lion hunting season and lions theoretically are protected. In the past two years, however, four lions that were deemed "documented livestock killers" were killed by officers of the Navajo Nation Department of Fish and Wildlife (NNDFW), which operates its own predator control program. One of these lions was a female with two cubs that are now being rehabilitated by an outside organization in hope of reintroducing them back into the wild. The body parts of the lions that were killed were given to medicine people to be used in ceremonies. These lions were the first of their species known to be killed—legally or illegally—in at least fifteen years and probably much longer than that. In recent years NNDFW has experienced an increase in complaints about mountain lions, which it attributes to a rise in the lion population. But no one really knows if lion numbers are increasing or if other factors are at play. Again there is talk by NNDFW officials of initiating a study to learn more about this most secretive of predators.

In distant times, when food was scarce and the Navajo people faced starvation, they often turned to the mountain lion for their very survival. In those times of hardship Navajos sought out kills made by cougars and they would then feast upon those kills. The Navajos who utilized this food source believed that the mountain lion purposefully made these kills and left the meat behind for the people to find and consume—a gift from a fellow being that possessed far superior powers, and certainly far superior compassion, than those usually demonstrated by its human counterpart. In such cases it was proper etiquette for the hungry but appreciative Navajos to respect the mountain lion's generosity by not eating all of this meat—which they referred to appropriately as being a "pity portion"—but rather to leave some behind for their benefactor.

In earlier times the mountain lion protected, provided for, and shared its wisdom and power with the Navajo people. In return, the lion asked for and received only understanding and respect. It was a relationship that worked well for both Navajo and lion. Today throughout its range—including on the Navajo reservation—mountain lions are under siege. There are valuable lessons to be learned from the beliefs and practices of the earliest human inhabitants of this land in terms of how we—all of us—relate to the natural world and our fellow beings like the mountain lion. Hopefully we will one day be wise enough to learn and utilize this traditional knowledge.

LION STORY

Montana — This author and his dog reel from a surprise encounter with a legendary "catamount."

A mountain lion once chased my dog Colter down an old logging road. It was in the summertime and we were just out hiking, climbing the mountain above the cemetery. Colter got a ways out ahead of me, galloping-charging up that mountain, only a year old, but already as powerful as a drafthorse, as graceful as a thoroughbred — and after a little while, I heard him yelping excitedly, as he often did when he flushed a grouse by accident.

His nose was forever leading him to grouse.

There was a silence, after that. I assumed he was chasing the fly-away bird, an act I hoped to discourage, and I shouted, "Colter, leave it!"

I was standing on the slope of the roadcut above the old grown-over logging road. Presently I heard the cyclonic thump-pattering of his feet coming my way, and within a second or two he whizzed right past me, moving faster than I'd ever seen him move. His ears were flopping and his tongue was hanging out and his yearling's long legs were scrambling as fast as those of a cartoon character — and I thought, Man, he really wants that bird.

Such was his speed, the fury of his legs churning, that he could not control his flight; he kept tripping over his chin, his body propelling itself faster, it seemed, than his legs, so that he would sometimes cartwheel; though even in his cartwheels he kept cruising along. He raced right past me — "Colter *leave* it!" I shouted again — and he gave me this wild-eyed look that seemed to say, What do you think I'm trying to do?

And then right behind him came the lion, bigger than I realized a lion could be, looking like something transposed from Africa, gold as a grizzly and as large, so that at first I thought that's what it was — head as large as a basketball, and huge-shouldered — until I saw the long tail floating along behind it.

It was easily twice as large as any lion I'd ever seen. I read later that occasionally males can get up to 250 pounds, so I guess that's what this one weighed, though in the shock of the moment, I would have estimated the lion's weight to be about 600 pounds. He glided past me with a strangeness of locomotion I had never seen before — it was as if, with his long easy strides so slow compared to Colter's churning rpm's, the lion was floating, drawn along on some magic carpet. Looking slightly down on the lion from the roadcut embankment, I could see every huge muscle working, reaching and pulling.

The lion was gliding right behind Colter, like some huge floating Chinese dragon in a parade, or a lazy kite string at the end of the furious dynamo of Colter. At any moment it seemed to me that the lion could have reached out its big paws and pulled down this small brown screambug rocket of a dog, but the lion seemed to be made momentarily curious by the little twitching nub of Colter's tail.

The lion passed right over my shoe tops. I could have netted him with a six-foot dip-net. There was some shadow-part way down below me and not at my core that weighed the option of being silent and letting this play itself out and, maybe, everything would somehow turn out okay—but that was just the dry shell of a consideration, having no more life to it than the husks of insect skeletons you find clinging to the sides of buildings in the early summer, and braided into the nests of birds.

A boy loves his dog; a man loves his dog. "Hey," I said to the lion, or something like that. It was only half, or three-quarters, of a shout. "Hey, asshole, leave my dog alone."

The lion glanced up at me, clearly surprised as it cruised past, but it kept on gliding. Dog and lion disappeared into deep grass twenty yards away—there was a single yelp, then silence—and I could see through the tall green grass the motionless shape of that big lion.

I was afraid he had Colter down—had perhaps broken his neck with one swat—but I held out the thin hope that Colter was only in shock, and that I yet might somehow be able to claim him and carry him, entrails trailing down the mountain and into town, and get him stitched up and doctored and put back together again.

I picked up a chip of shale about the size and density of a deck of playing cards and advanced slowly toward where I could see the lion in the grass.

The lion turned and looked at me, and my first and immediate realization was to understand how easily one of these creatures could, by itself, kill a 700-pound elk.

My second impression or realization was that the lion was staring at me with perhaps the purest distillation of scorn I have ever encountered. Still I advanced, yelling at the lion, trying to work up a bravery and anger that just wasn't there, and which, by that cat-scorn look, the lion knew wasn't there.

But I could see the lion thinking, too. I could tell that there was just enough uncertainty about things—the surprise of my appearance into the equation—for the lion to be wondering if he had not somehow blundered or been lured into a trap.

The evidence before him—a pale trembly stick-figure advancing upon him with a lone handful of dirt-rock, then pausing and staring at him—clearly did not support this hypothesis, but that was the only thing, the only thing in the world I had going for me:

107

the uncertainty, that brief revelatory surprise, of my unplanned appearance. Hopefully to such an able assassin as this big lion, the lack of control in any area of his mission would be grounds for canceling his mission.

I stood there, gripping that dirt-wad, calling the lion names—hurling words at him. He did not look away from me, nor did the degree of his scorn, the intensity of it, lessen.

I saw my dog! As if only now coming into focus, I saw Colter sitting on his haunches, knock-kneed and straddle-legged, panting, tongue hanging out. If scorn was the lion's essence, in that moment, I would have to say that bewilderment was Colter's.

I grew up in Texas, reared as a child on the Fred Gibson stories of noble dogs such as Old Yeller and Savage Sam. For long moments I entertained the belief, the longing, that under no circumstances would Colter let anything happen to me—that now that he was turned around and had the situation figured, he would in no way let that lion attack me: that he would do whatever it took to protect me. Me, the one who fed him, and protected him.

The three of us formed a long flat dangerous triangle, with the lion at the apex. I called to Colter, whistled for him to slink past the lion and come stand by my side, so that we could make a stand, two against one—or, better yet, to get the hell out of there—but Colter only looked at me with that same panting incomprehension. He just sat there, looking all goofy, and with the heavy awareness of the responsibility of adulthood, or some other awful thing, I realized that not only was I going to have to take care of myself in this fracas, but my dog, too.

It was in the end all just a little too weird for the lion. After more scanning, he turned and walked off into a dense tangle of blown-down lodgepole—the bulk of his body taking up as much of that little logging road, it seemed, as a tractor-trailer, and yet after he was gone, he was really gone, vanished, and when I went over to collect the panting brown sack of my dog—I had to lift him as if gathering up a limp stuffed animal—I peered into that jungle of blowndown lodgepole fully expecting to see the lion crouched in there, repositioning himself and recalculating things for a return attack.

But he was gone forever, gone from our lives anyway, though for the next couple of years stories would come from off that mountain of other hunters who'd had encounters with him. In future years enough stories would come from the same area so that it was not even like a myth, but a certainty: that if you went to that spot on the map, that lion was going to fool with you. God knows what he ate: mule deer and elk, I suppose. One hunter even had several little cubs chase him in that area one time, so that surely those were his progeny. They were so young they were barely able to run yet, but came snarling and spitting at him anyway, little kittens. He left, too.

Another time the big lion snuck up on an elk hunter, who turned and saw the giant staring at him, crouched, at a distance of about five yards. The hunter hurled a steel hatchet at the lion and struck it—like tossing an empty aluminum can—but the lion turned and ran back off, and disappeared.

He hasn't been seen, or noted, for a couple of years, but it's hard to believe he's not still out there. Though maybe too he was already old when all that was going on, so that now, soon enough, he is motionless—that big basketball of a skull gleaming bright on a hillside somewhere; bone-sharpened teeth pearl-polished and still open as if protesting or snarling at even the rising and setting of each day's sun; the lion's long ship of bones relaxing and slipping, dissolving from its previous order, a vertebra or two tumbling down the hill; a femur rotating awkwardly in a way it never would have in life; the lion's eerie round skull looking somehow so alien and, to our way of thinking perhaps, superior to the skulls of so many slain deer in the garden of bones on that hillside around him.

But even in that repose, even in that transition from full-muscled grace to loose-boned chaos, I think a grace would return to the magnificent old lion. I think yarrow would bloom through one of the huge perfectly round eye sockets one year. In the case of that lion's magic, anything is possible to imagine: maybe twin yarrow, from each orbital, or twin penstemon, like prayer flags in the wind. As if those bones were incapable of being too-long disassociated from grace or beauty.

Perhaps for a hundred years, or longer, deer on that mountainside avoid even the location of those bones, as if believing they might yet reassemble themselves and leap up again into headlong gigantic flight.

We have no sure ways, really, of knowing anything. Our hearts and the blood of the centuries that our hearts pump know so much more than what we can read or experience in a lifetime.

What I suspect happened with Colter and that lion—though I cannot be sure, can only guess or imagine it—is that Colter, with his excellent nose, caught wind of a grouse, and was working it, and got to it at the same time the lion was stalking it, and that the grouse flushed; and that the lion, angered, and surprised, chased Colter.

Quivery-legged, afterward, Colter and I hiked on down the mountain, glancing over our shoulders often.

We passed through the cemetery on the way to where the truck was parked: passed beneath those shady, ancient tamaracks.

He was one year old, that year.

SOUTH DAKOTA COUGAR

South Dakota — A scientist, using a vacant summer cabin as a blind, is treated to a rare viewing of a mother cougar and her three cubs.

My interest in wildlife grew out of a childhood passion. I always felt a deep connection to the wild. I knew I would spend my life continually seeking to know more about it. But when I saw a BBC film called *Puma: Lion of the Andes,* my focus became clear. In the documentary, the brilliant filmmaker Hugh Miles tracks and documents a female puma in the wilds of southern Chile. There are no settlements nearby and, in time, the feline comes to accept his constant presence and his ongoing observations. Eventually, she gives birth to a litter of kittens, and we see the family's early life play out before our eyes. I was completely mesmerized from beginning to end. At the time, I had no way of knowing just how much this film would impact my life; I just knew I needed to know more about this amazing animal.

A few years ago I was working on a cougar research project in the Black Hills of South Dakota. One afternoon I got a call from the groundskeeper of a remote, vacant summer camp. He informed me that he had discovered a fresh deer carcass, presumably killed by a cougar, in the woods surrounding the camp.

That afternoon, I drove to the location and found the deer, covered almost entirely with leaf litter and twigs, the trademark concealment of a cougar's kill. Although it was winter, snowfall to this point had been minimal. Patchy areas of snow revealed evidence that a family group—a female and her kittens—had been feeding on this kill the night before. At that time, the kitten-sized radio collars I had ordered had been delayed from the manufacturer but I was told they were due to arrive any day. So, in the meantime, I decided to see if I could observe this family group and determine just how many kittens there were. I asked the groundskeeper for permission to stay the night in an old cabin that was less than thirty feet away from where the cougar had cached her kill. As luck would have it, a full moon scheduled for that night was likely to increase my chances of seeing the family returning to the kill after dark. I placed an old VHF radio collar inside the remains of the deer with a magnet strategically balanced on the battery. When the family returned and began to feed, the battery would simply roll off and the collar would start transmitting a silent signal. Inside the cabin, the receiver would begin to beep, alerting me of their arrival.

It was a frigidly cold night so I suited up in my warmest winter gear, jumped into my sleeping bag, and placed my receiver on the floor next to the couch and waited. Shortly after nightfall, the static from the receiver was replaced by a "beep, beep, beep." The female and her kittens had arrived. Within moments, I could hear the crushing of bones and the sound of growling kittens fighting over food.

To keep my presence unknown, I needed to move with great care inside the cabin. I slowly peeled back my sleeping bag, climbed out, and began to make my way to the window. The old wooden floor proved to be the greatest test to my patience. With each step, the floor groaned under my weight. The window, not six feet from the couch, seemed miles away. However, I knew that if I let my excitement get the best of me, the cougars would hear me and quickly disappear into the night.

I finally managed to reach the window. Standing to one side, I slowly moved the curtain just enough to peek out with one eye. To my great disappointment, the family was invisible, hidden by the shadow of the cabin in the moonlight. I prayed that soon my eyes would adjust to the light and I would be able to make out at least some figures. I waited, thrilled just to be listening to the sound of meat and bone being eagerly devoured by the cougars. More time passed and the family remained hidden, so I resigned myself to the notion that even without seeing them, this was still a great honor indeed. After all, I was able to remain undetected in the presence of a female cougar and her kittens as they fed on their kill less than thirty feet away from me.

As the night grew bitterly cold, I decided to return to the warmth of my sleeping bag. I crept back to the couch as slowly as I had moved away from it and crawled inside my sleeping bag. Eventually, sleep got the best of me and I began to doze off, all the while being serenaded by the sounds of the cougars. I believed I would be hard-pressed to find an experience to compare to this in the future. I was dead wrong.

Some time had passed and I awoke suddenly to the sound of a soft "thump." It took me a moment to get my bearings and remember where I was. Then I heard it again . . . "thump." I sat straight up in my sleeping bag as I realized the sound was coming from the deck that surrounded the cabin on two sides. All at once I knew it had to be the female and her kittens. I slowly crept to the door that bordered one side of the deck. I gradually moved the curtain that covered the window on the top half of the door. As it was on the opposite side of the house from the deer carcass, the deck was flooded in moonlight. I stood and listened but heard nothing. I began to wonder if my imagination had played tricks on me and I had not really heard anything at all. Then, all at once I saw a small shadow coming out of the darkness in the distance and moving up onto the deck. It was one of the kittens. It strolled right past the door less than two feet from where I was standing. Before it even registered in my mind, another one followed behind it. Then, in the dirt just on the other side of the deck, arrived the mother and one more kitten.

113

As they moved past me, I realized I needed to make my way to the window that bordered the second side of the deck. If I thought my patience had been tested the first time I had to creep across the room, it was nothing compared to this. I was even more impatient this time as I slowly, quietly crept across the room. I finally made it to the window and peeked out to see that the mother and the final kitten had now joined the other two on the deck. The mother lay down in the middle of the deck with her back to me. I could see that her belly was large and full. As she rested there her tail repeatedly curled up and then flopped back down again. Near her, two of the kittens were pouncing on one another, rolling around the deck, a single ball of fur. Then the third kitten started to swat at the mother's tail. Within moments, its interest turned, and the kitten began to growl playfully and bite at its mother's neck — the mother quickly put a stop to this.

The kitten then retreated and turned its interest to a small strip of wood that had fallen off one of the window sidings. Soon, the three kittens were batting the wood back and forth across the deck. At one point, two of the kittens jumped up on a picnic table and resumed a wrestling match. They eventually tumbled off the table and back onto the deck. The mother continued to lie there contentedly, tail slowly curling up and down, periodically licking her front paws and staring off into the darkness.

The family remained on the deck for the better part of a half hour. All of this took place within ten feet of where I was standing. The observation ended as abruptly as it had started. The mother got up, took a long stretch followed by a deep yawn, jumped slowly from the deck, and disappeared with her kittens into the night.

To this day I still pinch myself when I remember that evening. I know I shared a truly rare and unique honor with Hugh Miles as I silently observed these incredibly fascinating creatures, gaining an unobtrusive view into the secrets of their lives.

MY BUSH SOUL, THE MOUNTAIN LION

Colorado — The power of an animal appearing repeatedly in dreams calls forth deep examination of the lessons we may glean from them, illuminating the connection humans share with our wild brethren.

Over the years many animals, both wild and domestic, have called and spoken to me in countless dreams as well as in real life. I have been blessed to have lived in the Rocky Mountains where encounters with wildlife are frequent. But it was my dreams of powerful "fierce creatures" of the wild that got my attention and focused it on the transformative significance that animals have had in my life.

Two of the most memorable and meaningful of these dreams occurred when I was on a wilderness retreat in the late 1980s. In order to reconnect with the Earth and my own heart, I did a six-day and six-night solo among the wild cliffs on the west side of the Sangre de Cristo Mountains on the northern edge of Crestone, Colorado. I have found that solo time in the wilderness is one of the most effective ways to get out of my head and back into my body so that the wisdom of the unconscious may speak. The vivid animal dreams recounted here convey the power of that experience.

115

As I made my camp among the cliffs on the first night, I noticed that I was laying my bivouac sack and sleeping bag right in the middle of an animal trail. I had to remove abundant deposits of mountain lion and deer droppings in order to have a relatively smooth and level place to sleep. Since I'd been warned that I was in mountain lion territory and was alert to the possibility of a visit by one, I was not surprised that I was visited by the local cougars in a dream that night. But I was surprised by the content and direction of the dream.

> A mountain lion cub padded into my camp in broad daylight when I was sitting up in my sleeping bag. I had no weapons. I sat very still, not daring to make a sound. The cub was sniffing curiously around the foot of my bag when its mother followed it into camp.
>
> Knowing that there are few creatures fiercer than a big mother cat defending her young, I realized how futile any attempt to defend myself would be if she decided I was threatening her cub. I was paralyzed with fear, frozen, barely able to breathe. But as I sat there, I slowly realized that it was an honor to be joined by the cub and its mother. I felt admiration for and kinship with them. Caught between the conflicting emotions of fear and love, I concluded that if the mother cougar wanted to take me, there would be nothing I could do, so I would give her my life. I relaxed, surrendered to the situation, breathed quietly, and just watched.
>
> The mother mountain lion had sauntered in and stretched out on the ground several feet away from me, seeming, as cats do, not to take any notice of me. She was the picture of nonchalance. Following the cats' etiquette, not wishing to challenge her, I didn't look her in the eye. We simply sat in each other's presence for a while without making eye contact. Then a strange thing happened – the mother cougar turned into a woman, and the woman became my friend. Suddenly we were going to a party together.

This dream turned out to be the first in a series of dreams about mountain lions that I had over a period of several years. The next animal dream occurred a couple of nights later, after I had settled into the retreat and was feeling a deep level of relaxation and contentment.

> *The dream began with a scan of the outside of a sterile institu-*
> *tional structure, a building that expressed a linear mindset, like*
> *one of the schools I had attended in the 1950s. The basement*
> *of the building was crowded with indigenous women – Native*
> *North American, Latin American, Black African, Australian*
> *Aborigine, and others – all dressed in traditional costumes*
> *and speaking very fast in their native tongues. They were very*
> *agitated and were gesticulating and expressing their feelings*
> *vehemently. Among these women were two other kinds of crea-*
> *tures, huge serpents and large cats. King cobras, pythons, boa*
> *constrictors, and other enormous snakes were coiling and hissing*
> *and arching in strike poses. Black panthers, cougars, jaguars,*
> *leopards, tigers, and other great cats were pacing and snarling*
> *and roaring. None of these beings were in conflict with each*
> *other; they were all feeling the same entrapment in this awful*
> *structure and expressing their frustration. The basement was*
> *seething with the tremendous energy of these women, snakes, and*
> *cats. They wanted out.*

When I awoke from this dream early in the morning, I thought, *No wonder they're all riled up, being trapped in that institutional structure. I would be, too.* I fell asleep again and forgot about this dream until I was back at home.

One night toward the end of the retreat I lay in my sleeping bag unable to sleep for most of the night. There was a different energy this night, the first I was able to stay awake long enough to see the stars. A lightning storm thirty miles to the west in the San Juan Mountains—no thunder but great, silent flashes of diffused light—lit up half the sky every few minutes. This lasted long into the night. Between these bursts of white light I gazed at the Milky Way arranged brilliantly across the crystal-clear sky. It was the time of the new moon and the week of the annual August comet shower. Between the lightning flashes, shooting stars enlivened the deep indigo sky. I felt incredibly blessed to be able to witness Nature's own spectacular fireworks.

After counting twenty shooting stars, I surrendered to a sense of wonder. I became aware for the first time — though this was my fifth night out — that it was far from silent among the cliffs. In the background, the rushing sound of the creek below echoed off the rock walls. But there was something else. I began to sense a kind of music in the world surrounding me. Even beyond the echoes of water and the sounding and resounding of the stars loud with light overhead, there was the music of the life around me; I became aware of the life around me. It wasn't the rustling of animals, it was more subtle. I thought about the cougar dream and the fears I'd had that first night. Now I felt surrounded by a world that was not only friendly but singing to me, inviting me to a party, letting me in on its secrets, giving me a glimpse of the magical quality of our living Earth, the living quality, the power of ancient rocks and trees and stars. Perhaps this was the party the cougar mother was leading me to.

It was not until much later, years later, that the full meaning — and irony — of the basement dream sank in. In the short term, I recognized the images of the dream. There was a strong presence of feminine energy, not only among the women but also among the snakes and cats, associated as they are with the feminine in Western tradition. The indigenous women represented to me the primal feminine wisdom that is intimate with the Earth and knows the secrets of Nature.

The big snakes represented powerful transformative energy. I had been sympathetic with snakes since childhood. During a field trip when I was ten years old, I had been thrilled at the smooth sinuousness of them as they wrapped and coiled themselves around me. In later life I had outgrown and shed my psychological skin several times, like a snake. Images of the Goddess often have snakes coiling around Her arms. The snake is an ancient image of the soul emerging from within the Earth.

In my adult life I had been fascinated with big cats and also had small cats as my companions. The big cats represented power, grace, beauty, and a strong maternal style of leadership and responsibility. I also recognized that those powerful archetypal energies were trapped within my Self in a rigid, sterile institutional structure — the intellectual mindset that structured my life. I realized that my rational, linear ways of thinking and living were repressing the instinctual and intuitive elements of myself in the unconscious. I saw that those powerful forces "in the basement" were unhappy being imprisoned within that structure and that they could be a strong creative force in my life.

However, I could not foresee at the time the extent to which the dynamic image of this dream would mark the beginning of a long rite of passage, a journey of the soul. It was a turning point after which the process of change would take on a particular character. I couldn't appreciate the elegant simplicity with which this dream would symbolize the path that was to unfold, because I couldn't foresee just how many structures in my life would be transformed from the "basement." Both the cougar dream and the basement dream turned out to be prophetic: it was the animals that slowly, gently led me to a deeper place of heart and grounding within myself.

Once animals had gotten my attention, I began to consciously follow the passion I had always felt for them. That is, I consciously attended to the coincidences in my life that involved animals and looked for their significance. *The Medicine Cards*, by Jamie Sams and David Carson, became a helpful reference for interpreting the gifts and powers of North American animals according to the Native American tradition.

Many psychologists, particularly Jungians, have studied dreams about animals and have recognized animals as messengers of the wisdom of the soul. The Latin root for animal is *anima*, which variously connotes breath, mind, and soul, as well as the feminine aspect of a man's personality. An animal is literally a being with a soul. *Anima*, as in "animating," is the enlivening factor. Indigenous "animistic" traditions perceive the entire natural world as alive and imbued with soul. The *anima mundi* is the great maternal soul of the world, conceived in various images and known by many names in the diverse cultures of the world.

The Christian tradition was complicit in giving both animals and indigenous peoples a bad name, projecting onto them uncontrolled carnal appetites, beastliness, and savagery, which were actually more characteristic of immature "civilized" humans than of animals and indigenous peoples. However, depth psychology is helping to restore animals to their helpful, healing role in the human psyche and is also validating the wisdom of indigenous cultures.

I once asked Marc Barasch, author of *Healing Dreams*, what he had learned about animals in dreams during his research. He said that animals are a primary phenomenon in dream life: "Very often in healing dreams they have extraordinary presence, very lifelike. They don't seem symbolic. You almost have to encounter them on their own terms rather than reducing them to icons or some symbolic factor in the psyche."

He also mentioned that indigenous cultures discuss animals in dreams as the "animal familiars" or "totem animals." I asked Marc if he could clarify the term "familiar." He responded that "it literally means you have a connection with a particular animal and it becomes your totem animal. You aren't supposed to eat it or dire things will befall you. It's living its life, it's your 'bush soul.'"

He continued: "What kind of message does this have for us in this culture? We are embedded in Nature. What happens to the natural world happens to us and what happens to us happens to the natural world. This kinship system that included the animals and that is still reflected in our dreams is a very important thing to acknowledge. A lot of people who have had no more contact with animals than a petting zoo still have extraordinary encounters with totem animals in dreams—bears and mountain lions and eagles. We think it's a new age cliché—you know, like 'What's your totem animal?' I think that these are spontaneously appearing in people's dreams, and I'm fascinated by it."

Often the animal is the carrier of the wisdom of the body, the carrier of the other qualities that we need to incorporate in our lives. James Hillman has a wonderful discussion of this. He says maybe you'll dream of a fox or maybe a weasel, some animal you don't much care for, because very often our animal dreams are not about these great, noble predators but about the smaller, more opportunistic animals. These are giving us a clue to some essential part of our personalities that perhaps we haven't fully acknowledged as natural and as our own. So if we dream about the fox, maybe we have a sharp nose, maybe we're clever or even a little bit sneaky. But that quality is not something we should simply reject as something immoral but rather acknowledge that maybe we have a trickster quality and should use this animal image or this animal feeling as a touchstone for our own growth and wholeness, a more complete way of being in the world.

Because they continued to appear in my dreams, I became particularly interested in mountain lions, a cat par excellence. *Puma concolor* is known variously as mountain lion, cougar, and puma. Long before I talked to Marc, I suspected that, in coming to me in dreams, the mountain lion was a totem animal for me. According to the Medicine Cards, Mountain Lion is a difficult power totem to have: "Mountain Lion medicine involves lessons on the use of power in leadership . . . [and] the use and abuse of power in a position of influence. . . . If Mountain Lion has come to you in dreams, it is a time to stand on your own convictions and lead yourself where your heart takes you. Others may choose to follow, and the lessons will multiply. . . . [T]he first responsibility of leadership is to tell the truth. Know it and live it, and your example will filter down to the tiniest cub in the pride."

When I read this, my hair practically stood on end. I had been studying issues of leadership and power for nearly a decade. I had also been engaged for several years in a painful struggle to maintain my integrity in relationship to my mother. As her health deteriorated, she had become increasingly authoritarian, trying to manipulate me in a confused attempt to retain control over her life. Also, only a couple of years before the retreat in the Sangre de Cristos, I had left a job where I had observed disturbing abuses of power that affected many people. I had stood on my convictions, spoken my truth, and led myself where my heart took me, which was into the movement to protect the rainforests. I was in the middle of editing *Lessons of the Rainforest* when I went on the retreat where I had my first mountain lion dream. The mountain lion brought to consciousness the two themes of "speaking truth to power" and leading myself by following my heart, both of which have been prominent in my life since that retreat.

The next mountain lion dream repeated a theme similar to the basement dream. In this, as in the dreams to follow, there was only one cougar.

> *I was in a large, imposing university library, which in some ways resembled a cathedral. It had a very high ceiling, large leaded windows high on the walls, and a hushed, reverential atmosphere. The reverence in this case was for higher learning, something to which I had been dedicated all my life. An elderly man in a tweed three-piece suit and wire-rimmed glasses approached and politely asked if he could help me. But I suddenly became distracted by the mountain lion standing by my side and twitching her tail. The cougar was looking toward the elevator from which a white-haired lady in a pink suit emerged with a miniature white poodle on a leash. I felt a rush of adrenaline as I feared the cougar could attack and eat the poodle, right there in the university library. I sent a psychic message to the cougar: No, please don't. Not here. The cougar stayed where she was and I breathed a sigh of relief when I realized that she would honor my message. Then I woke up.*

In retrospect this is a marvelously rich and ironic dream, although it took me awhile to appreciate it. Here again was the intellectual structure, a bastion of civilization. When I had attended the Universities of California at Riverside and at Berkeley, I had worked in the libraries of both institutions. Although the library in the dream did not look like UC Berkeley's library, the atmosphere was similar to what I had experienced as a student. Clearly, there was something in my ego structure that had been imprinted by such structures of learning, symbolized by their architecture. My wild, instinctual aspect was confronting that ego structure—in fact, my very sense of identity. However, I was not ready, apparently, to allow my wild self to create havoc within that structure.

In this dream the mountain lion was out of the basement, on ground level, and "behaving herself" from the dream ego's point of view. She did not indicate any intention of attacking the poodle, other than the twitching at the end of her tail, but I projected that she posed a threat to order if she chose to attack the dog.

The poodle leashed to an old lady represented to me the domestication of my instinctual nature by my intellect, by civilization, which the mountain lion was calling attention to. I was uncertain of the lion's allegiance to me and whether I could control her, but by the end of the dream I began to feel that this wild creature could be trusted. Meanwhile, the question of whether the librarian could help me was left hanging. It was now a question that I began to address consciously. In fact, I became aware that the dominance of my intellect over my instinct and intuition was a painful theme in my life.

In subsequent mountain lion dreams, the situations involved people with whom I had conflicts. In each of them the cougar appeared benignly at rest in the midst of a human drama. He was there for me, like a reminder, an ally and protector of my deepest inner truth. In the course of this series of dreams, which numbered five in all, I became more and more comfortable with and trusting of her, until I finally recognized her as my familiar, my "bush soul."

That is not to say that we had a cozy, cuddly relationship—she was never my pet in these dreams. Rather, she was a powerful ally with whom I had a respectful relationship. I do not recall ever touching her in these dreams, but there was a psychic connection between us. She was the guardian of my true nature, my integrity. She bequeathed to me the confidence and courage to set boundaries and stay true to myself in my waking life.

In the last mountain lion dream, which was six years after the initial dream, I was on staff at a Buddhist meditation retreat center in the Colorado Rockies. This was the dream.

A woman who claimed to have healing powers was adjusting people's auras. Other members of the staff were standing passively in line to have their auras adjusted. I was not in line but was observing from a distance. The woman doing the adjusting came up to me and looked me in the face. "Aren't you going to have your aura adjusted?" she asked, as if it was something I should do.

"No," I said, "I don't have my aura adjusted by other humans. I get my aura adjusted by my mountain lion," gesturing to the cougar standing next to me on the right, "and by contact with the Earth." Then I leaned over and touched the Earth. I woke up, amazed.

I hasten to add that nobody I knew claimed to "adjust people's auras" nor has anyone attempted to overtly. However, the dream very accurately framed for me a decision I was compelled to make at the time. It showed me that power relations do adjust people's auras, for good or for ill. That is, when someone has power over others — as is the case in every human family, group, organization, and society — the use or abuse of that power affects everyone's psychic field. In the world of unenlightened people, power usually corrupts, and the effect on the collective psychic field is negative. When challenged to prove that he was enlightened, the Buddha himself did not appeal to human authority. Rather, he touched the Earth and said, "The Earth is my witness."

I didn't think I was enlightened, but this dream signaled for me the end of a lifelong struggle to prevent my aura — my psychic field — and that of others from being adjusted in a negative, disempowering way. Without being fully aware of it, I underwent an internal shift and entered a new phase of my life in which I no longer had to deal directly with abuses of power. Many confining institutional structures, internal and external, fell away. I gradually let go of judgmentalism and intellectualism, and simply sidestepped power struggles as I stayed true to myself and remained a free agent in my own life. It was around the time of this dream that ecopsychology began to call me, and it eventually became my calling.

I have come to believe that what all animals and ecosystems deeply need and desire for the health of their souls is to be free agents in their own lives, and especially free of domination by humans. The mountain lion has been my subtle companion and guide on this journey, and photos of her on my walls have kept her presence alive in my life.

The meditation center also had a resident wild mountain lion, observed by a number of staff members over the years, although I never saw it myself. I wanted very much to have the honor of seeing her (or him) in person but was granted the next best thing. One spring I was thinking about this mountain lion, wondering if it was still around because no one had seen it for a year. I hoped it continued to grace the land and decided to go out and look for signs.

As I walked up the trail to the top of the valley, in the direction of the national forest, I silently asked to be shown tracks: *Please let me see a track so that I will know you're still here.* Within a couple of minutes, just after I had reached the top of the trail, I felt pulled to my right off the trail. I walked slowly, scanning the wet ground where snow was still melting. Much of the ground was bare rock or a gravelly surface, where I would not be able to see any traces, so I concentrated on the soft ground and snow patches. Very shortly I saw it: a large, clear front paw print in the mud, with a fainter back paw print behind it. There it was—definitely a mountain lion track—like an answer to my prayer.

"Thank you! Thank you!" I said aloud, feeling joy and gratitude that the spirit of mountain lion was still with me.

I continued my walk along the Forest Service road that borders the center's land, walking slowly and continuing to invite contact. I knew that people had been attacked by mountain lions along the Front Range of the Rockies. But I also heard it was possible to scare them off by raising your arms and making yourself look bigger, shouting, throwing rocks, and fighting back if necessary. Cougars do not expect their prey to fight back. I also carried a walking stick, which— if used to hit one—I'd heard can be sufficient to scare off a cougar.

However, because of my deep sympathy and connection with these creatures, I felt no fear and certainly had no intention of hitting a mountain lion with my walking stick. I reasoned that mountain lions are usually afraid of people, with good reason, and go out of their way to avoid us. I also doubted one would be interested in me as food. It's usually juveniles who have left their home territory that attack people on the trails near populated areas. These are inexperienced hunters who are hungry and don't know the dangers posed by humans. But I was far from the Front Range and was in the home territory of a particular mountain lion. There were miles of national forest, uninhabited by people, adjacent to the center; and the surrounding forest offered plenty of other game.

I strode along the road with a light heart, keeping my senses open and looking for more signs. As I neared the fence that marks the western boundary, I saw another sign. In the middle of the road, only a few feet within the boundary, was a large pile of deer droppings. On top of it was another pile—mountain lion scat, all big and hairy and white with crushed bone.

I burst out laughing. It was as though this sign, deer and mountain lion scat, was there to remind me that my entire journey with the mountain lion as my bush soul had begun when I had removed deer and mountain lion scat from my camp the first night I dreamed of the mountain lion. Of course the deer and mountain lion weren't thinking of me when they left their signs on the road, but those signs had a powerful significance for me, nonetheless. "Thank you again!" I said. "I see that all's well. Thank you!" Feeling relieved and reassured by these signs, I turned back and returned to my office.

Although I couldn't have put it in these terms at the time, the spirit of the mountain lion began my initiation into the deeper secrets of the psyche, which are inseparable from the magic and mystery of Nature. After many encounters with wild animals, my unconscious intuition has gradually become a conscious conviction that the soul of the Earth, expressed through her sentient creatures, responds and speaks to human souls who are open to that possibility; for there really is no separation at the soul level. And that is what Nature and all her creatures are dying for us humans to learn.

LION HEART

*Wyoming – For this author, following an outfitter on a hunt, a differ-
ent understanding of cougar pursuit emerges.*

High in the Wind River Mountains, the
Whiskey Basin cups the sky, a bowl-shaped plateau rounded out
by glacial melts and frost heaves and the repeat pounding of seis-
mic shifts. This is Marlboro Man country, and, like the cougars who
dwell here, it is expansive, mysterious, vast. It is a favorite place for
Rocky Mountain bighorn sheep, for elk and mule deer, and moose.
And because of these congenial vegetarians, it is also a favorite for
raven and cougar, black bear and coyote, for wolves. They speak
each other's language, these animals, their tracks a conversation in
competition, in survival. The trails of hooves and paws, the concen-
tric circles of magpie wings alighting in the powder, the crunch of
snow mixed with blood, the drag marks of a mule deer's body all
quietly tell the stories that shape and define this small slice of the
animal kingdom.

Then there are the tire tracks, the grooves made by the blades
of a snowmobile slicing the powder with an inorganic mechanical

127

perfection, the hoofprints of several packhorses mashing the trail to an unrecognizable slush of travel in a single-file line, the frenetic wandering paw prints of dogs combing out across the snow in search of a scent trail. Here, hunting the Wyoming backcountry, one creature is always following the next, and so it was that I followed a hunter, a cougar outfitter, a houndsman, a father, a husband, up into the mountains to film his point of view on why he takes people out to hunt America's greatest cat.

Mid-March was late in the season to be tracking cougars, but a generous snowfall the night before had him itching to take his dogs out to track and possibly shoot the eighteenth and final lion that could be killed here, in one of the twenty-nine legal lion hunt areas in Wyoming. We met just after first light. As the outfitter saddled up the horses, a small group of bighorn sheep watched from the shadow of hulking roseate cliffs two hundred yards away, their heavily horned heads cocked slightly to one side as if trying to understand our kind.

Hunt Area 18 sits within part of the basin and encompasses a sliver of the Wind River Mountains, our trail rising an abrupt one thousand feet in the course of just one mile. I struggled to cooperate with my horse's labored balance, hunching low over his withers and cooing soft words of encouragement as we climbed the hill together, his body at a sixty-degree angle to the mountain. We all struggled, and then the outfitter told me flatly to get off the horse. "The trail's too steep and the snow is slippery. Horses will lose their footing." Sliding off the mare's back in one fluid motion, he clucked twice, threaded the reins through the space between his palm and his fingers, and started to walk. "Hold on to his tail and just let him drag you up," he suggested, advice that went against everything I've ever been told about being around horses. Knowing better, or thinking I did, I trudged along behind in a seemingly coordinated combination of several steps forward and one long slide back, giving my horse fair room to kick.

Within two hours, we crested the northern rim of Whiskey Basin and the outfitter glassed directions I thought we'd never be capable of covering with horses. The dogs, who had bawled and paced and run circles around each other up the mountainside out of sheer anticipation for the trail, were now far gone, their barks bouncing from canyon to canyon, haunting the quiet of the wilderness. Having led more than two hundred cougar hunts, the outfitter could discern the direction of the dogs' calls. Pointing out a set of tracks, his finger traced them to a rift in the forest. "Come on, it's getting late," and with that, he turned and headed in the direction of the tracks.

The tracks broke off in two different directions. Were there two cougars or just one that had backtracked to then go another way? Were there two consorts—a male and a female—traveling together? Was it a mother cougar with a nearly grown cub about to break away on its own? We made our way in the direction of the bawling dogs.

To catch a rainbow on a dry fly is an exhilarating, rewarding experience, an act of fishing that seems pretty fair for both trout and fisherman alike. But to move through a stand of trees and encounter a cougar, trapped by dogs and nearly hidden within a tangle of branches, felt sacrilegious. A sense of intruding pervaded, my stomach tightened, a gut reaction that told me we were treading on sacred ground, stealing a part of the great cat's wildness, exploiting its vulnerability up there in the tree, taking advantage of the very instinct that has allowed this animal to survive thousands of years. Cougars have evolved to take to trees to flee wolves, their wild competitors of yore, and this innate good sense to seek refuge remains in their souls today. What they have not learned to anticipate, however, is that after the dogs comes man, man with a crossbow or rifle or pistol. And then there is no way out.

How to describe *shame*? I felt embarrassed for the animal, and, averting my gaze from hers, I fixated on the task at hand—steadying the camera, framing the shot, the lens somehow separating the reality I found myself in. I rolled the tape and let the outfitter tell his story. He explained how he loves cougars, never wants them to be gone, but believes that they must be controlled, their numbers "kept in check," that man must prevent the carnivores from eating all the deer and elk and sheep. It was an explanation, a justification of sorts, that I had heard before, only not here in the land of the wild things, not under a puma no more than twenty feet above us, not as the dogs continued to whimper and bay and run circles around the base of the tree. He told me that if the cat was a female, if she was nursing or had cubs, he would let her go. At the time, I had no idea. Cougars are difficult to sex, and although outdoorsmen will claim that you can discern a male from a female based on the length of their stride and the width of paws as seen imprinted in the snow, the truth is that to know you must see the males' black guard hairs, just beneath the base of the tail.

The cougar remained expressionless except for one single thread of drool hanging from her mouth, her weight teetering on a branch just high enough to get away from the dogs. Right to left, left to right, she shifted the weight of her body between two large, seemingly boneless rear paws, finally settling onto her haunches, the left paw resting on top of the right. The cat didn't seem to care that she was standing on a short, sharp snag. Her forelegs held on to the upper branch, leaving her entire underbelly, paler than the golden brown of her coat, exposed.

The last thing the lion must see is the sky, the heavens, the protective cover of the forest canopy as she falls from her perch, all silence except for the whip, snap of branches cracking one by one, quickly in succession, her entire world turned upside down.

Some cougar outfitters advertise that when you go with them on a hunt, you'll get to eat the lion's heart right at the spot where you kill the cat, that its warmth will penetrate your body, and that your body and its body will become one. Perhaps this adopted ritual is meant to bless you and bless the animal, although I don't really believe so. I believe it is so the chill of the killing won't haunt you, that the cat's eyes, wide and green, won't sear their image into your dreams, that you won't awake with night sweats and that you'll still be able to go out into the forest tomorrow and see the sweetness, not the aftermath of the hunt, not the heart, so small it fits snug into your palm, not the heart, velvet soft and still beating, not the heart, still remembering, still warm, still wild on your tongue.

A LION, A FOX, AND A FUNERAL

Colorado – A renowned professor of animal behavior makes an intriguing find near his own home as a cougar and a fox ritualize survival and death.

Because my living space encroaches on the terrain of mountain lions and many other carnivores — including coyotes, red foxes, and black bears — the likelihood of meeting one of these beasts is fairly high. Red foxes entertain me regularly by playing outside of my office or on my deck. I once had a young male black bear casually stroll onto my deck and try to swat open a screen door that leads to my dining room, where I happened to be eating dinner at the time. He stepped back when he couldn't get the door to open, looked at me, and just hung out until I went to the door and asked him what he thought he was doing. He continued to look at me, sort of shrugged as if he couldn't care less about my being there, and strolled off and rested for about an hour under a hammock near the house below mine.

I've been lucky to have many such unplanned encounters with various animals, for nature doesn't hold court at our convenience. Much happens in the complex lives of our animal kin to which we're not privy, but it's a truly splendid moment when we're fortunate to see animals at work.

Mountain lions, like black bears and foxes, also visit my home with little or no hesitation. They seem extremely comfortable sharing my home range with me, having habituated to my presence over the years. And technically I was the one who moved into *their* home. Somebody redecorated the lions' habitat by building my house smack in the middle of their living room.

It's not surprising, then, that I've had some very close encounters with my feline neighbors, including the time I almost fell over a huge male as I walked backward to warn some of my neighbors of his presence. On a warm July day in 1993, I arrived home thoroughly exhausted after racing my bicycle for three hours in Denver, only to learn that a mountain lion had killed a deer up the road from my house and was still lurking in the neighborhood. Some of my neighbors had small children, so I hiked up the road to tell them what had happened, each step causing my fatigued legs to ache.

When I got to the first house a few hundred yards west of mine, I saw my neighbor on his porch and yelled to him that there was a lion around and that it would be a good idea to keep his kids home. Just as I turned to walk to the next house, I came face-to-face with a large male lion—so close that I could have touched him. Of course, I was terrified and ran up the hillside, in my clogs, yelling all the way, "There's a lion here, there's a lion here!" The lion just stood there watching me run, thank goodness. Later I learned that he had stashed his kill, a large mule deer buck, down below where I'd made his acquaintance. Luckily, I didn't cross the path between him and his catch. I'm sure that's why he didn't chase me—that and the fact that he had a full belly, having just eaten, we later estimated, about twenty pounds of fresh deer.

At a later date, when I told some people what had happened to me, some had the audacity, though they were well-intentioned, to tell me that it was stupid of me to run. They informed me that it's best to tell the lion who's boss by yelling and screaming and shaking your fist or some object—like a tree branch—at him. As a field biologist who had studied coyotes for years, I of course knew that it was best to intimidate a lion, not run from him or her. But I must say that when I looked the cougar in the eye from about two feet away, instinct took over. Fleeing trumped remaining and trying to convince him that I wasn't scared. I was scared. I think that if I hadn't been dehydrated from my bike race earlier that day, I'd have peed my pants. Had I done so, I suppose it would have been interesting to see the lion's reaction. Of course, with his keen sense of smell, there can be no doubt that the lion knew that I was quivering inside, regardless of my serendipitously empty bladder. I remember going to sleep that night imagining a headline in the local paper saying something like "University of Colorado Carnivore Expert Who Ran from a Cougar Gets Maimed — What Was He Thinking?" Now that would have been hard to live down.

A few years later I met another lion and discovered much about nature that I'd only read about. There's so much we don't know. Late one Friday evening I was driving up my road and saw a large tan animal trotting down toward my car. Thinking it was my neighbor's German shepherd, Lolo, I stopped and stepped partly out of my car to say hello, only to hear Lolo barking behind me as I came face-to-face with a male mountain lion. He stared at me and then walked off. I jumped back in my car, slammed the door shut, peeled out, drove home, and walked to my house with all my senses on fire. I was really scared, although on reflection not as frightened as I'd been when I'd met the lion on my road years ago.

Lolo made it home safely as well, and the next morning my neighbor told me that he'd found a red fox carcass, so I went to look at it. The fox, a very healthy looking male, clearly had been killed by the lion by a bite to his neck, but most of his body was intact and partially covered with branches, dirt, and some of his own fur. It looked as if the lion had tried to cover his prey, perhaps thinking that he'd go back for a meal later. I checked the carcass the next morning and it was still partially covered and unchanged from the day before. The lion hadn't returned.

Two days later, at about 6:15 A.M., I headed out to hike with my canine companion, Jethro, having waited until there was some light so we didn't encounter my lion friend again. I looked down the road and saw a small female red fox trying to cover the carcass. I was fascinated. She was deliberately orienting her body so that when she kicked debris with her hind legs, it would cover her friend, perhaps her mate. There's been a family of foxes near my house for more than a decade and I assume she was related to, or at least a close friend of, the deceased. She'd kick dirt, stop, look at the carcass, and intentionally kick again. I observed this ritual for about twenty seconds.

A few hours later I went to see the carcass and indeed it was now totally buried. I uncovered it and saw that it had been decapitated and partially eaten. I felt incredibly sad, trying to imagine what it was like for the fox as he ran from the lion, got caught, and then killed. Did he think he could outrun this large and tenacious predator? As a student of animal behavior, I am motivated in my own research by questions like "What is it like to be a given animal?" and "What does it feel like to be that individual?" Because I've spent decades studying animal emotions, it was natural for me to empathize with the fox and imagine that he must have felt incredible fear as he tried to outfox the lion, perhaps looking for possible escape routes that the larger animal couldn't follow, or running here and there, cutting small circles that the lion might not keep up with. Although I find it almost impossible to step back and look at events like this with total objectivity, as many a scientist would do, I do see them as reflecting cycles of life in the natural world. So, although I surely feel for the fox, I also marvel at the predatory skills of mountain lions and other highly evolved "natural-born killers." Killing for food is how they make their living, so someone has to pay the price for being at the wrong place at the wrong time. Nature is not always pretty, and lions should not be blamed for killing their food. That's the way it is. Having run from a lion myself, though, I have to say that it's certainly easier to identify with the fox.

No one I have spoken to—including naturalists, people who live among wild animals, and professional biologists—has ever seen a red fox bury another red fox, and very few have seen a mountain lion kill a fox. However, as I was making my final revisions to this essay, a neighbor of mine told me that he'd seen a red fox "flying across his porch." Seconds later, he saw a mountain lion in serious pursuit of his early morning snack. I'd seen the lion about thirty minutes earlier, just above my friend's home. What's also interesting is that although I frequently see red foxes around my home, they've been rare this spring. And three times in the past few weeks I'd sensed a lion nearby. In the past, whenever I've sensed the presence of a lion I saw one later. You just know they're there, you can really feel them lurking about. And if we know they're there, so do foxes and other animals who spend far more time and energy avoiding these magnificent predators.

As I discuss in my book *The Emotional Lives of Animals*, we know that individuals of many species hold rituals for those who have departed, saying their good-byes in their species-specific ways. I've observed a magpie funeral, llamas and otters grieve the loss of friends, and gorillas hold wakes. I don't know if the female fox was intentionally trying to bury her friend, but there's no reason to assume she wasn't. Perhaps she was grieving and I was observing a fox funeral. I have no doubt that foxes and other animals have rich and deep emotional lives. Back in 1947 a naturalist on the East Coast saw a male fox lick his mate as she lay dead. He also protected her quite vigorously. Perhaps he too was showing respect for a dead friend.

JOAN FOX

HUNTING AT NIGHT

Washington — In this short story, Jhonna reels from the loss of an unborn child. While contemplating another pregnancy, she takes a hard look at her husband and how one story he tells about a half-dead cougar may forever haunt her.

"Look at the deer," he said, pointing out the window. "Would you just look at them all." He put his hand on her knee. "How many do you think there are?"

Jhonna's arms felt heavy. She thought of lifting her hand and placing it over his, but didn't. She looked at his hand, her eyes held by the blue veins under his pale skin.

Matthew took his hand off her knee and put it back on the steering wheel. Jhonna was listening so hard the night seemed to tremble around them. She cracked her window, wanting to feel the cool wind. She was so tired her thoughts came to her as if they were dreams.

Last year she had been pregnant for seven months. The entire time of the pregnancy and for months after the induced stillbirth, she had felt this tired. Jhonna thought of the diaphragm she had used only once since then. Now it was kept in the cedar chest, pink and creased as an ear.

Sometimes she forgot and allowed herself to hope that she was pregnant. Mainly Jhonna felt withdrawn, almost isolated from hoping, and so from Matthew and the ordinary events of their lives. As of today, she was fifteen weeks late. She was allowed and supposed to hope. But she approached that thought with dread, as though it were a terrible job awaiting her.

Matthew slowed down some, then took his eyes off the road.

They both looked into the field. Below the horizon, between the night-blackened trees and the starry sky, deer fed on grass. Their large ears twitched and twisted distant from their bodies. "And just think of all the fawns," he said.

She didn't say anything, just looked out the window.

"Jhonna. Think we'll see any bucks tonight?"

"Matthew, there aren't any little baby fawns out there in the field," she said, without having heard him ask about the bucks. "It's too late in the year for them."

Jhonna spoke slowly and carefully. Often she called her husband "Matt," especially when he did not please her. When she said "Matt," her voice became lower.

The wind pattered in through the slitted window. Jhonna raised her arm, ran her hand through her hair. Her fingers caught on new tangles. He slowed down. "What is it?"

Her voice sounded different to herself, almost fearful that nothing was going right. He steered the truck to the side of the road. The engine made a sound like taking a breath, then he turned it off.

Matthew twisted his body; one hand stayed on the steering wheel. He put his other arm around Jhonna and pointed with that hand. The full moon shone over the trees and fields. The moon was bright and stayed in her eyes even when she closed them.

She looked where he was pointing. Blinded by their headlights, a possum weaved off the road onto the shoulder. Matthew turned off the lights. While her eyes adjusted, Jhonna bent over, out from under his arm, and tied the laces of her shoes, then she stepped out onto the road's gravel surface.

"Got the blanket?"

"Yeah," she answered. "Let's try down near the creek."

They walked down the grassy slope. The moon was rising, and they had no trouble seeing. Their shoulders and backs were warm. A wetness brushed their shins and ankles.

Jhonna wished the possum crossing the road had been a porcupine. She watched her feet kicking through the dirt as if they were eating up the ground. The moon's light shadowed her steps into triangles, aligning her body and the earth. Jhonna felt her heart thudding, new blood circulating through her body. She lifted her hand and put her fingers on the quill earrings she'd made last week: dangling loops with blue and red beads setting off the eggshell-like sheen of the white and black quills.

"Last time I was down here, I saw a huge one," said Matthew. Jhonna didn't say anything; her finger pulled the circle of her earring.

Matthew wanted her to go to the clinic in Colville and set their minds at peace. He'd been teasing her, saying he would drive her there, and all she had to do was pee in a cup. He was right, Jhonna knew, and they wouldn't have to wait for long. Just like last time, the clinic could tell them the results almost right away.

They separated under the trees: ponderosas, white pines, and larches. Even under the trees they had no trouble seeing. They walked around a ponderosa whose trunk was bare of branches until the top, where its branches and needles fanned out against the sky. Jhonna put her hand on the bark as she circled around the tree.

Matthew and Jhonna walked up an incline. At the top railroad tracks shone under the moon. Down on the other side of the embankment was Pierre Creek. Eventually the tiny stream from the north flowed into the Columbia above the Grand Coulee Dam. They stopped in the middle of the tracks and stood on the ties.

"Look how the moon lights up the rails," said Matthew. Jhonna nodded her head and started walking up the tracks. "It lights them up for miles," he said. "Look how far away."

He put his hand on the back of his neck and rubbed, pressing down hard. The rails shone, a silver spine stretched over the land. He looked down to the darker ground where they were going.

Behind them, the tracks wound through the trees, snaking to the left, then disappearing in a curve to the right. He heard something, perhaps an animal stirring, and stood motionless for a moment, watching the tracks.

Ahead of him, Jhonna stopped. He turned and walked along the ties to her. "Oh," she said, holding herself, her arms crossed over her stomach below her ribs.

On the tracks was the body of a large deer, a doe halved at the stomach. It was late in the year, yet the doe had been pregnant. Now the night air congealed its blood. It was the worst thing she had seen in a long time. She could not stop staring.

Matthew had been in Wallace, Idaho. She'd driven herself to the doctor, aware she had not felt the baby moving for almost a full day. The doctor waited for Matthew to arrive before inducing labor. Jhonna's baby had turned so the cord had strangled him. He fit into the tiniest casket. The doctor kept saying it was a one-in-a-million accident. The doctor had said other words too, words put into phrases to give Matthew and Jhonna hope. She never felt brave or strong enough to remind herself of those words, much less to believe them.

Blood was all over the ties and the tracks. She rubbed and pressed her hand over her stomach, fought the urge to retch. Matthew wrinkled his nose. The odors of iron and blood mixed with the cooler scents of grass and trees. The engineer wouldn't have tried to brake, even if he had seen the deer and had had enough time. No train could have stopped in time, he thought.

"Must have been the eight-o-nine through Island Rock." She had started, hearing his voice. He tapped the dead animal with the toe of his boot.

"Guess so," she said. She handed the blanket to him and stretched her arms wide over her head. It felt good.

They looked at one another and started walking down to the water, on the trail that cut through the underbrush.

Jhonna followed Matthew down the slope and into the trees. She concentrated on following him. He was still towheaded, like a toddler. Jhonna liked his large forearms and the way he didn't always swing his arms when he walked, as if sometimes he just forgot.

She heard the creek and there was the scent of water. "Here it is."

"It's a bit lower," Matthew said, looking down.

They decided to cross. The small rocks made clacking sounds when they stepped and lifted off them, then sucking sounds settling back into the mud.

Matthew and Jhonna turned left, walking upstream, and came upon a moose. Jhonna's heart beat faster at the sudden presence of the animal. The moose's face was lit by the moon. She saw the whites of its eyes before it turned away through the trees. She looked for a calf, not wanting Matthew or herself to come between it and its mother. Apparently the moose was alone. She heard its feet crushing the thicket after she could no longer see the moose, or tell where it had gone.

She could not see Matthew as he moved ahead of her through the brush. Again she remembered the sight of the deer. But seeing the moose had reminded her of another thing, and she shook her head, deliberately remembering that.

She was young when her father had taken her fishing. They had left home hours before sunrise and whenever she woke they were still driving. After driving for almost a full day, they reached the Grande Ronde, a tributary of the Snake River, in the southeastern corner of the state. Jhonna helped her father set up camp and then, as the sun lowered, her father fished upriver, moving farther and farther away from her. Cries of birds echoed across the sheer walls of the canyon. The river was dark blue. On the other side, a cougar with two cubs stared at her from the trail cut into the canyon wall.

Jhonna and the cat had watched each other until the cougar nosed her cubs and moved away. Staring at the cougars across the darkening water, Jhonna had felt something mysterious and special connecting them. It was because they were alive at the same time, and breathing the same air, but it also was beyond that. She never had forgotten that moment, not even when her father had come back and yelled at her for staying in the open after dark.

She was glad to have a memory from when she was a girl. She felt again how, despite her father's reprimand, she never had been sorry: so many important things seemed to happen in the darkness.

"Jhonna," Matthew whispered, "over here."

She breathed deeply and stepped over some rocks, remembering how the cougar had stood over her cubs, protecting them.

Matthew unfolded the blanket so it would be easier to throw. She put her hand out to touch his wrist, but he moved away. There was some vaguely formed question she wanted to ask him, but she remembered not to say anything aloud just then. She started walking faster, keeping up with him.

"Hey, hold up." He said this softly. They both peered through the trees. First they saw the beady eyes. A porcupine moved into the small opening formed by the trees.

Watching the porcupine slowly walking closer, she held Matthew's hand tighter for a moment and almost closed her eyes. The porcupine turned to run away, but Matthew threw the blanket over it. At the last moment she saw the porcupine puffed up, ready to throw its quills.

"Quick now," he said. The animal's feet began to push past the blanket edges.

Kneeling on the ground, she tried to push and keep the porcupine under the blanket. A foot kicked wildly against her palm, and for a moment she felt its nails.

"Oh no," she said, and pushed harder.

Her face felt hot. We need him, she thought, don't let him get away.

"Careful," Matthew said. "You got it."

She grabbed part of the blanket from him. Their hands touched, and he smiled at her. The porcupine made dry, scurrying sounds as it tried to escape.

Matthew and Jhonna continued to hold the blanket edges pressed against the dirt. The corner Jhonna held down was worn and fraying; through it she could feel pine needles on the ground.

From beneath the blanket came the furious sounds of the trapped animal. Its entire body thrashed and kicked, moving inside the blanket, trying to make its way out.

Still they held the blanket pressed to the dirt. Jhonna saw one paw held against the earth as the porcupine went momentarily still. The paw had a large pad and neat nails.

"We'll let you out," she said softly.

"What'd you say?"

"Nothing. I just don't want him to get away. And we don't want any quills broken."

The blanket stretched tightly over the animal. Matthew and Jhonna looked at each other and in one movement stepped back. They squatted on the ground next to one another, several feet from the animal.

She watched as Matthew put his hand on a tree to balance himself, and for a moment she felt that anything, not just the day-to-day events and plans of their lives, was possible. She smiled at him. She didn't feel tired anymore. The porcupine stopped its furious struggling.

"Let's just wait," Matthew said and nudged her. She fell against him. He gently pinched the fat on her waist.

"Ow." Laughing, she pushed him to the ground.

She is bigger, he thought, and pulled her down with him. His hope that she was pregnant ached in his chest as if he had been holding his breath for a long time. The feeling gradually slipped away through the dark spaces of the trees, as dew might, expanding to fill the air. He tightened his arms around Jhonna. She was laughing and trying to get away.

"Got you," he said, then playfully bit her nose. "I know how much you like that."

"No," she said, "what I like is breakfast in bed."

"That'll get you fat." He leaned closer.

"Hope so. You should hope that, too." There was a flatness in her voice. She remembered Matthew saying that they had to sell the one mare. The mare had not foaled; Matthew doubted she ever would.

She saw his vision of how he wanted things to be on the patch of land they had saved for, bought, and now worked. The mare who had not foaled did not fit. She imagined he worried too — about how to pay for the doctor, how to pay for delivery; mainly about her carrying a baby to term. Still, even if he worried, she thought most of the burden fell on her. She put her hand on her stomach. Everyone, even strangers, would want to know how she was doing, how she felt, what she was thinking. When the baby was due. She felt a sudden weight of cold air. She shivered.

"Hey look," he said. They watched as the porcupine shook off the blanket.

"All right," Matthew grinned. "A big one."

She never looked at the porcupine after the blanket came off and before it ran away. What would it look like after it threw so many quills? She couldn't think of exactly why she never wanted to look.

"You gather those in the blanket." She said this to him as she collected quills from the ground. Each quill was toothpick-size and almost weightless, a hollow black-and-white tube, especially sharp on one end. The quills reminded her of the bare, featherless pointed ends of feathers. Some quills were opaque, dense and strong looking; these quills were of that type. She held up several to the moonlight. The quills were white with just a touch of black at the tip. Both ends were pointed and sharp. Coarse hairs from the porcupine were wrapped around many of the quills. She did not bother separating those out. As she squatted, she twisted her back, to the left, to the right. The moon was almost straight overhead; still she threw a shadow on the ground. Jhonna wanted to see; she didn't want to miss a single quill. Those still tangled in hairs from the porcupine were slightly harder to see.

Brushing off her hands when she thought she had all the quills, she sat down cross-legged beside Matthew. He gathered the quills in the blanket, piling them together in the same direction. She put her quills with his.

"This is a good-sized bundle," she said. Picking out some stray quills, she settled them on top. Jhonna touched the quills lightly, avoiding the sharp ends.

"The most ever from just one," he said.

"Bess is going to give us a good price," she said, brushing off her hands again, then wiping them along her pants.

"She will, she will," he laughed. "Last time I was over there her perfume turned my stomach."

"She's a nice lady, Matt."

Bess lived on the reservation, near the Okanogan county line. She made jewelry out of the quills, earrings like Jhonna's, and sold them, mainly to tourists at pow wow and to Indian traders. Jhonna thought Bess did pretty well for herself and for her family, which was large.

Matthew was right; these were the most quills ever. But she remembered her lost baby and wondered if she fit into Matthew's vision of how things should be. Her mind, once started worrying, could not stop. She remembered him choosing and buying the mare. Finally she remembered hearing him say that he would sell the animal and why.

She leaned back on her heels in the dirt, watching as he separated the quills from the pine needles, then arranged them in rows. She felt a tenderness toward him. But she could not relax into the feeling. *He doesn't have to worry like I do*, she thought, *he just takes things for granted*. Her tenderness gave way to a kind of anger.

Her hand pressed her belly. She wanted to distance herself from Matthew. She stared at the side of his face, his hands as they moved, lifting, setting down the quills. Then she looked for faults in him.

A story of his that he always told came to mind. Just last week he'd told it to a hitchhiker. Rather than listen yet again to the story, Jhonna had either watched the hitchhiker's face or looked out the window while Matthew told about the time he and his cousins had come upon a cougar caught in a trap, weak, but still alive.

They brought the cougar home and put it into an old suitcase. Then they set that suitcase on the side of the road and waited, watching from the roadside ditch. Matthew and his cousins wanted to prove that Indians from the reservation were stealing from them. This suitcase was their proof and revenge. Before long, a car pulled up. Matthew leapt from the ditch and waved them on. "We're waiting for Indians," he hollered. Matthew always said the suitcase was finally picked up by the Indians who had been stealing. He said they were drunk and hardly stopped long enough to brake. Their car sped away, took the next turn, and right about then, the Indians opened the suitcase. Matthew and his cousins heard the Indians yell, the cougar's high roar like a scream, and the tires squeal, all at once.

Whenever Matthew told that story he laughed, and his face went soft and young. Thinking about the story and how Matthew always laughed while telling it made her feel sick.

Matthew told people he was a pacifist, and he was. He had signed special papers about it, years ago. He hunted to keep food on their table, but if there was a new war, he would not go and fight in it.

The story, she reminded herself, was from when Matthew had been younger. He hadn't thought as much about the world. Still she was uneasy.

"Matt," she said, "some people from Cheweiah called, said they saw our ad for firewood and that we deliver anywhere."

"Well, we got time to drive it down—and drop off the quills too," he said. "Hey, things are falling into place."

She realized he was feeling optimistic. For months and months, and even now, after trying his best to comfort her, Matthew would go outside alone to grieve over their lost baby.

She put her hand to her stomach. She wished she could speak to him, and that he would say words in return to make her believe she was pregnant and that the baby would be born. She did not speak. Instead she imagined him laughing while the Indians' car screeched to a halt.

But I've never seen him be mean to a soul, she said to herself. *That crack about Bess and her perfume was as mean as he ever got.* Now he was leaning over the blanket, arranging the quills. Jhonna breathed out, hard, through her mouth. She brushed stray hairs off her forehead. Maybe he was right; maybe things were falling into place for them.

"I guess things are getting better," she said. "Ever since we got those chickens."

Matthew had helped some people tow their car from a roadside ditch. In return, they had given him several hens and a rooster. He had made a gift of them to Jhonna, surprising her.

"Yeah," he said, "they're our good luck."

She almost smiled at him. She thought of lying in bed and listening to the chickens scratching, clawing, and climbing their way up the screen window, all this right outside their trailer. And the fence they had broken.

"Matthew, you think we should fix that fence? Maybe I should try to build another one."

"I thought we decided to just forget it."

"Yeah, but I don't think it's the dog that's been eating the calf's food. I think it's the chickens."

"You shouldn't be doing any extra work now," he said. He looked at her. "Just in case," he added.

Her heart started beating faster, harder, against her stomach. She leaned over, as if picking up more quills from the ground, so he wouldn't see her face.

Matthew had finished rolling the blanket around the quills. Now he tucked in the blanket edges so the bundle was secure. He smiled, thinking that things were starting to pay off. Maybe they would make it on their own; for now it would be nice to buy the hot water heater without having to take one hundred and some dollars from his paycheck.

He did construction, in season, the kind of work that paid well, when there was work. Most days of this summer he had been driving over to Idaho, about seven hours each way, to work on the construction of I-90 through Wallace. But he hoped someday the land would support them and their children, all their lovely, beautiful children. What he wanted was to be independent, self-reliant—he wanted no part of a society he thought was too violent. Matthew thought Jhonna understood, that basically she agreed with him.

They were building their house, and he was worried. Already it was late summer and he didn't have the plumbing finished. He wanted to get as much done on the outside while the weather held. He hoped this would be their last season in the trailer, and that next year at this time the house would be finished, and they would be inside it.

Jhonna was walking slightly ahead of him. He smiled when he saw how tightly she held the bundle of quills. He imagined their children running through the rooms of the house to go outside, those moments he and Jhonna would enjoy being inside.

Matthew and Jhonna walked to the creek and re-crossed it. Matthew thought of driving with the vents in the cab open, the whoosh of foxtails spitting through, sucked in from the night. The cab would smell fresh and sharp, like the smells of gasoline and grass. He lifted his arm and shaded his eyes from the moon's glare.

Jhonna shifted her bundle and grabbed his arm. Flaring through the trees, somewhere below the tracks, a flickering light showed. She whispered. He didn't hear, but walked faster. The trees swayed in forms flat and black against a fire.

"Oh Matthew, someone left a fire. Just left it. All the way out here."

"This fire could go running wild," he said.

Jhonna pictured the fire pushing through the forest, knocking down trees.

They approached slowly. The air was stiffer near the fire. For the first time the night felt cold to them. Waving her hands over the fire, Jhonna glanced to where she had put down the bundle of quills. Tiny sparks flew up, lit up the ground, and sizzled on the dampness. Matthew brushed one from his pants.

They poured dirt on the fire, enough to put it out. Jhonna's eyes watered from the smoke as the dirt funneled through her fingers. She wiped the powdery stuff from her wedding band.

Picking up the bundle of quills, she rearranged it in her arms. They walked up the railroad embankment and re-crossed the tracks. Matthew looked up and down the rails, staring at their beauty in the moonlight. Walking down, Jhonna thought of the dead deer.

"Where was the deer — that dead deer?" She shook her head. "I didn't see it on the tracks."

"Someone must have got it," Matthew answered.

The moon was higher, the air cold and damp. Jhonna thought of the deer's legs tied together to make it easier for carrying, the crushed unborn fawn. She wondered who would have taken it, and she felt like crying. There were certain things that shouldn't be taken away.

"Let's get out to the road," she said. As the moon rose, tree shadows the color of ash lengthened.

She wanted to get home, be home; even sitting in the truck would be nice, she felt. She stopped walking. She remembered the fire. She agreed with Matthew: the world seemed a dangerous place. She saw a baby, theirs, helpless, trusting.

"You okay?" he asked. In the dark, Matthew's eyes were deep blue, almost black.

"I was just thinking," she answered. Jhonna started to walk and then stopped, turning to Matthew. Her hands tightened on the bundle of quills, then slowly relaxed.

It was as if she did not see Matthew, but saw him instead as the person who had been in his story about the cougar and the Indians. And the story was all tangled up in a vision she had about their dead baby, a baby caught and captured in a compartment from which it could not escape alive. But this was hazy, and even if she could have put this half-formed thought into words, she never would have told it to Matthew. Or to anybody.

But there was something she hated about that story of his. And she felt something hazy and undefined just beyond her reach, hiding as if it were a quarry — some knowledge about stories and why they mattered. She almost reached for Matthew, as if to ask him for help in seeing what she longed to see. Instead, she stayed silent and waited.

The stories people told mattered. From each story their baby could either learn about the world, or else only learn about its parents, those fears or smallnesses that were particularly theirs.

The stories you tell matter, she wanted to explain to Matthew.

But on her way to saying aloud what she had just figured out, she realized that the stories you tell yourself matter even more. *I can never have a baby,* she had told herself, *I'm not going to have a baby.* Obviously. "His dying was a one-in-a-million accident," the doctor had said. *And I am the "one,"* Jhonna thought.

She put her hand on her stomach, right below her heart. That had been the place their baby used to kick. Her other hand again tightened around the bundle of quills.

But that was a story. A story she had told herself, had made herself believe. Why? He had said something else, too. He had said there was no tissue damage, that she could hope for an ordinary pregnancy and safe delivery of a healthy baby. *Yes,* she said to herself, *I can. I can be a good mother. A good mother. I can be a good mother.* She let her hand move over her stomach and almost she smiled. Jhonna started to walk and then stopped, turning to Matthew.

"Matt, I don't want you to tell that story anymore."

"What story?"

She stared at him in reply.

"The one about the Indians?"

"Yes," she said. "It makes you sound mean."

Suddenly the bundle of quills was unbearably heavy. She handed them to him.

"With the cougar?" he said. "It's just a story."

"Not anymore, and it makes you sound mean." She paused for a moment, then went on. "In it, you are mean. When we have children, I don't want them to hear that story. Not the way you tell it. I want them to learn to be good to people."

I do too, thought Matthew, but he didn't say anything. The Indians who took the suitcase, they could've been Bess's brothers, people she knew. What would she think of that story?

Jhonna breathed deeply. That was what she had wanted to say to him, that you have to see beyond your own experience. She thought this but did not say it. Instead she started walking, as quickly as she could.

Matthew watched her plodding through the grasses. He wondered how angry she was, or if it was that she was tired. He remembered when she was pregnant before, how she would begin weeping whenever she was hungry or tired. His throat was dry. He hoped there was a can of soda or beer in the cab. Behind him the power lines were humming. He turned and saw them extending across the sky, lit by the moon.

He saw Jhonna stop at the fence. Against the wires her shape looked simply dark, vaguely formed. The barbed-wire fence separated the field and the road. He caught up to her, and they parted the strands for each other. She let go of the wires after he ducked through. Matthew straightened. They looked to the left, where their truck was parked farther ahead, off the road. The moon was out, but the road looked dark.

"I guess that story's getting kind of old," he said. He tried to laugh. "We are too."

"It just doesn't sound like you," she said. "It never did." She sounded tired. He looked at her face, almost didn't say anything.

"It was me," he said. "I was younger."

He remembered that day, how he had followed his cousins. He wanted to go fishing. Then they found the half-dead cougar. He couldn't remember for certain anymore what those screams had sounded like. He hoped it had been only the tires. His arms and neck felt cool. He stopped walking and looked at the sky. At the center the moon still burned. Only occasional stars could be seen around its light.

She was right. From the beginning he had felt bad for the cougar, though he hadn't let his cousins know. Always he told himself, even now, that nothing bad had happened to the people in the car.

It was he, though, who had stopped the people in the first car from taking the suitcase. He remembered himself hollering, his heart bursting with pride as his cousins whooped and cheered him. He felt almost sick.

He looked at the side of Jhonna's face. The moonlight made a pattern of her expression, showing her face as shadowy, then lit again, depending on her movements. She stopped walking. He saw how she put her hand on her stomach.

"Tomorrow we'll stop by the clinic," he said, "we'll find out for sure." He put his hand on one of her shoulders and rubbed it gently.

All night she had been looking for signs, especially after they had seen the doe on the tracks. Matthew's hand on her shoulder felt good. She remembered Matthew and herself working together to catch the porcupine, then gathering its quills.

"Yes," she said, "on the way to Bess's we can do that. We can tell her our news." She reached for his hand. They walked along the road, in the direction of the truck. Jhonna let her other hand rest on her stomach. She felt warm and alive.

Bess kept all her colored beads in plastic trays on shelves. When the sun came through the windows of her small house, each plastic section looked as though it held a glowing ball of colored fire. It was a beautiful sight.

Tomorrow, Jhonna and Matthew would deliver their quills in that light. They would not need to tell Bess a word. Jhonna's stomach was rounder; it was growing and getting rounder every day. Like something both escaping and showing itself for the first time, the situation would instantly reveal its truth to Bess. In the background, Matthew would smile, bundled quills in his arms.

A SHORT, UNNATURAL HISTORY

Colorado – A carnivore conservationist outlines the political history of America's greatest cat, explaining why commonly held beliefs may not hold true.

At the turn of the twentieth century, conservationists distinguished between what they deemed to be "good" and "bad" animals. Prey species, like young deer, were "innocent victims" whereas predatory animals, like pumas and wolves, were considered "ravenous" and "bloodthirsty." Important spokesmen, President Theodore Roosevelt and Dr. William T. Hornaday, director of the New York Zoological Park, telegraphed this message. It seemed neither could abide a predator. In 1901, Roosevelt held a record for killing the largest puma in Colorado until he was bested in 2001. Roosevelt's quarry came from Lyons, Colorado. If the conservationists couldn't tolerate a puma, just imagine the sentiments western cattlemen and sheepgrowers shared.

Surprisingly, the ethic concerning large carnivores has only changed in the last few decades. In the 1930s and 1940s, scientists like Aldo Leopold and brothers Adolph and Olaus Murie began to study carnivores and publish their accounts. Wolves and coyotes did not kill for mere sport, they killed for food, and they lived in family units. Leopold and the Brothers Murie helped to alter the discourse concerning predators, especially in the scientific community.

Ironically, during this period of biological investigation, Congress passed the Animal Damage Control Act in 1931. It required the agency then called the U.S. Biological Survey—now the U.S. Department of Agriculture's Wildlife Services—to "promulgate the best methods of eradication, suppression, or bringing under control" on both public and private lands a whole host of native carnivores, including pumas. The intent of this work, according to Congress, was to protect livestock and farming interests. The Animal Damage Control Act remains on the books to this day.

While the Muries and Leopold changed the biological understanding of pumas, one remarkable activist, Rosalie Edge, helped engage the public. In her firebranding pamphlets from the early 1930s, Edge condemned the U.S. Biological Survey for "inflaming hostility toward our bird and animal neighbors." She dubbed the agency "the United States Bureau of Destruction and Extermination" and complained that the survey's "methods" were "reckless, cruel and indiscriminate."

In her pamphlet "The United States Bureau of Destruction and Extermination," Edge wrote that pumas were "rapidly following the grizzly bear to extinction" because the survey not only spent "considerable sums to exterminate the mountain lion by traps, poison, and other methods" but also "inflame[d] the enmity" of pumas, which was "already too great," by "exaggerating" the "tales" of livestock losses. Edge aligned with the American Society of Mammalogists, which in 1931 dubbed the Biological Survey "the most destructive organized agency that has ever menaced so many species of our native fauna."

Beginning in the mid-1960s, western states ended bounties on pumas—that is, exchanging puma parts, often a scalp, for payment. At this dawn of enlightenment, during the radical 1960s and 1970s, western states finally began to regulate hunting pressures on pumas, with one notable exception—Texas. (To this day this hunters' paradise offers pumas no protections at all; even shooting spotted kittens is not discouraged.) By this time, pumas had largely been extirpated in the United States from the area that lies east of Interstate 25.

What were the effects of the bounty period? The number of cats killed in the West during the bounty period remains contested terrain among puma biologists. One school of thought holds that western puma populations were suppressed by bounties and the U.S. Biological Survey's 1920s and 1930s poisoning campaigns.

Others argue that actually, compared to present-day figures, few pumas were killed during the bounty period because of the lack of technology and limited access in hard-to-reach places in the unroaded and often impenetrable West. Because of poor record keeping compounded by the loss of bounty records through time, the full story will likely never be unearthed. Colorado, however, is an exception, where bounty data are excellent.

Colorado maintained a bounty on pumas from 1881 to 1965, with only a brief intermission from 1885 to 1889. Under Colorado law, puma hunters would turn in a puma scalp to the county clerk and sign an affidavit declaring the county where the animal was killed.

In spite of a $50-per-scalp incentive for bounty hunters, fewer than one hundred cats each year were turned in from 1929 to 1965 for money, for an average of forty-five payouts for cougar bounties each year. From 1997 to 2006, an average of 345 pumas were killed each year.

Today, pumas primarily inhabit the area from the West Coast to the Intermountain West. Except for California where sport hunting is banned, they are now hunted in record numbers. In ten western states (Arizona, Colorado, Idaho, Montana, Nevada, New Mexico, Oregon, Utah, Washington, and Wyoming), sport hunters killed 931 in 1982, reached a peak of 3,454 in 2001, and then dipped slightly in 2005 to 2,445. Texas does not track how many are killed by sportsmen.

From time to time, the media reports that intermittent pumas scatter to midwestern states. The Great Plains, however, act as a

Great Puma Barricade. While dispersing, pumas require cover such as trees or brush for travel and for hunting. Waterways such as the Platte River offer pumas travel corridors to the east, but the difficulty of establishing breeding populations in the Midwest comes from pumas' own dispersal tendencies. Young males typically travel further from the natal area than their sisters while looking to establish a home range. Also, males may have difficulties finding females in the Midwest, and thus establishing resident breeding populations may take some years.

Island populations of pumas have recently been documented in North and South Dakota. When those states discovered pumas in their midst, they immediately rectified the situation by setting draconian hunting quotas. In South Dakota, for example, all private landowners near the Black Hills can kill a puma, essentially resulting in unlimited quotas.

Many biologists claim that puma populations have rebounded, but the truth is probably as elusive as the puma itself. No historic baseline data exist, and even today, only a few subpopulations have been surveyed. Furthermore, the regulations that manage puma populations are inconsistent from state to state and based on arbitrary boundaries: hunt management "units," state and county lines, and other distinctions that make no sense to the wide-ranging puma.

So, how well are pumas doing now? Truthfully, no one knows. Pumas, after all, are cryptic creatures. But their highly secretive nature, although a challenge to researchers, is likely what has ultimately saved them from extinction.

THE SHIFTING LIGHT OF SHADOWS

Colorado – A late evening cougar sighting near the very human environs of a university tennis court sparks dreams, a "door to another world," as this author examines the idea of large carnivores in the context of Jung's archetype of the Shadow.

I'd seen ghosts of them now and then: the recently cleaned spine of a deer lying on a mountainside, bloodied ribs reaching up from the ground like arms trying to hold on to empty air; on another day, a carcass so fresh I thought it was an injured deer lying with its head on a rock. I began walking toward it but stopped when I saw the shiny dark flask of the stomach removed and placed prominently on a nearby rock, ravens beginning to gather above it. I thought better of my approach then.

I spent one winter tracking them for Colorado State Parks. That's when I learned that mountain lions crave fresh meat so much they will not eat the predigested stench wrapped in the stomach of their kill. Cats are finicky eaters. They carry the stomach away, like an offering to the needier scavengers. I also learned to walk very upright as I tracked. Bending down to, say, study some possible sign more closely was not a good idea. It would have turned my two legs into four, giving any nearby lion a familiar line of sight up my spine to my neck. A lion is generally stymied by the teetering, humpty-headed stature of two-leggeds—perhaps one reason why attacks on humans are so rare.

I always presumed I was in the presence of a lion when tracking. There are just too many cats in the foothills of Boulder, and too many signs. Still, during those six months of steadily following cougars, I never saw even the tail of a cat as it ran away, never saw a distant lion pacing on a far-off cliff or heard one caterwauling under the shivering Colorado stars, though nearby residents said they heard lions almost every night. No doubt, lions were watching me as I searched futilely with my human eyes—probably looked right at a cat—and never saw one.

I never thought a tennis court would be the place. Imagine the "What to Do If You Encounter a Mountain Lion Here" instructions. "Make yourself look big. Face the lion and don't turn your back. Never serve but always volley if served to. Avoid running for the ball; this could spur the lion's chasing instinct. Keep your eye on the ball. A lion could take direct eye contact as a full court challenge."

It would be pretty unlikely to see a wild cat striding across that smooth green surface where, earlier in the day, Edgar and George, vacationing from Texas, donned white shorts and tees and ran with their creaky, sixty-year-old knees, on spindly hairless legs, chasing bright yellow balls and calling, "Good shot, good shot, Cowboy."

But predictability is not any big cat's strong suit. My first, and only, sighting of the lions native to my Colorado home was on a tennis court in the Boulder foothills. I was staying in what I have come to call my office—a cabin I use in Chautauqua Park when I need a little extra solitude for writing. After work that night, I had walked into town with my partner for dessert; on the way back we were feeling good. We'd had some kind of gooey chocolate-caramel ice cream thing, a split of champagne—why not?—and we were, maybe, a little bit buzzed. We were certainly oblivious, but no less so than the average person coming home, unlocking the door, and entering the house every night. It's just one of those human tendencies. As we rounded the corner to the cabin, though, that common obliviousness vanished. Lisa stopped talking mid-word and tugged my sleeve. "Look," she said. I thought she was pointing to the silhouettes of two great horned owls sitting in the ponderosa pine. I looked up, but something pulled my eyes down. I saw it — in the spotlight of the green tennis court — a lion.

I've seen bears in the wild before and have often mistaken them for something else at first glance. My mind, an unfortunate stranger to wild animals, clicks on the bear cubs and says, "Hey, that's one huge dog," "one strange looking deer," "a very fat black housecat."

It was not that way with the mountain lion. It was unequivocally, distinctly, and deftly a lion.

Even though that recognition struck me with certainty, it was hard to discern the figure of the cat. I'd spent six months looking for this creature. I had begun to believe in mountain lions the way some people believe in God. I knew they existed, but I had given up finding anything other than circumstantial evidence. I never imagined meeting one in the flesh. Stunned, I watched the cougar cross the court, crouched, shoulder blades jutting from its back like the jagged slabs of rock it had emerged from. I guessed it was a male, weighing in at over one hundred pounds of pure muscle. Still, it looked afraid. It looked as if it knew it was in unfriendly territory. It prowled along a decidedly precise path, as if it had a specific place to go and regretted having to cross the tennis court to get there. Its massive head turned slightly from side to side as it slunk across the concrete, then leapt, all one hundred pounds of it — soundlessly — up onto the spectator's ledge. It passed between two houses and emerged onto the street, caught between the head-lights of a car and a group of teenagers.

It was anything but aggressive. It hunched down and away from the headlights, like a housecat confronted with a mighty vacuum cleaner. With the car clearly in its line of travel, it had nowhere to go, so it turned and followed the teens, walked within ten yards or so of them, and the second it saw an escape route, it vanished. I didn't see its escape route. Simply, the cat was there, and then it wasn't. My eyes couldn't follow it. No sign of it remained in its wake.

I wish I could say I walked quietly back to my cabin, let the whole event sink in. I didn't. I had finally caught sight of something I'd been looking for, something sublime. I was exuberant. I called out to the kids, "Hey, did you know there was a mountain lion right behind you a second ago?"

A boy looked over his shoulder. "What?"

"A mountain lion!"

The whole gang glanced back at me, then burst out laughing. "Right," one of them said. They went on about their nighttime carousing.

I couldn't sleep that night. I woke every hour or so, looked out to the tennis court. When I did sleep, I dreamt about the lion over and over. In my dreams, it was less shadowy, more familiar. It seemed at home there, in my sleeping brain where all sorts of impossibilities become real, where the reality of them vanishes in the light of day.

In Carl Jung's theory of dreams, the unconscious mind is layered. The most accessible layer is the personal unconscious. It consists of memories and repressed thoughts or experiences. The deeper, more complex layer is the collective unconscious, and its contents—the archetypes—are common to us all. A dream that strikes us with indelible power has likely risen up from the collective unconscious. In its logical extreme, the collective unconscious is not bound by time or limited to humans. It suggests that we are all one—a notion that in Jung's day had not been diluted by pop culture as it is today. It changed the course of psychological inquiry. Dreams, Jung said, are the doorway to the personal and the collective unconscious, and the degree to which we become individuated, conscious beings is equal to the degree to which we integrate the unconscious.

I can't say I understand the unconscious mind entirely, nor do I know what it would feel like to be fully individuated. But I know what it feels like to dream something powerful and indelible. The cat came to me like a dream, like a door to another world, a world so foreign and distant that I stumbled over the threshold of it; a world so familiar and integral to who I am, maybe to who we all are, that I longed for it. It was not a sentimental longing. It was the recognition of a necessity, not of a romantic accouterment.

One of the most well-known of Jung's archetypes is the Shadow. It is often misinterpreted as solely the negative side of the Self—the potential for each and every one of us to be everything that we fear in others: from self-absorbed and snotty, to liars, thieves, even murderers. And although all that unsavory stuff is true about the Shadow, the Shadow also holds within it all our internal repressed fears that are positive: the part of us that may be afraid of success, or of being loved, or losing our temper, or of the very daunting possibility of becoming whole.

It doesn't seem coincidental that the mountain lion is often called the Shadow Cat. It is nocturnal. It shows itself when most of the world is dreaming. To ranchers and owners of livestock, it is a thief. Cats are often seen as mysterious, not to be trusted. Even more often, they are seen as killers, and it is becoming more and more likely that because of this perception, they will be killed (and we, the killers).

It's the most natural response one has when confronted with the archetype of the Shadow. We see that which we fear and despise about ourselves manifested outside of us, and we seek to eradicate it. We view it as Other—unwanted and unnecessary.

But eradicating the Shadow, rather than integrating it, would mean a breakdown of the personality. And eradicating the mountain lion from the wilderness we all know as our history, our "collective unconscious," if you will, would cause a breakdown of what remains of that wilderness, to say nothing of the effects it would have, consciously or unconsciously, on the human psyche (which in Greek means "soul"). Annihilate all that you hate and fear, and it takes with it all that you love and desire.

If the world dreams, it dreams in the language of cats. It's not any more New Agey to say that cats are symbolic to Americans than it is to say the eagle is symbolic. If the eagle has come to symbolize some collective sense of freedom, the cat has come to symbolize solitary strength, self-awareness (awareness even in darkness), keeping to one's boundaries (in the way a lion holds to its territory); it symbolizes the heart of the wilderness we all need and desire — the wilderness that is shrinking beneath us, unconsciously, like a dream forgotten upon waking. Palpable, yet distant.

The next morning, when I went to check out of my cabin, I mentioned my sighting to Kathleen, the concierge. We'd become friendly since I began staying in the Chautauqua cabins, and it felt okay to speak to her about it. Still, as soon as the words left my lips, I wished I'd kept them to myself. I'd witnessed, the night before, a messenger from a place I hold to be divine — wilderness. True wilderness is pretty much gone now, but a remnant of it remains in something as sheerly and unyieldingly wild as a mountain lion.

As I walked downtown that morning, I knew my world had been shifted in the same subtle but certain way it shifts in the aftermath of an unshakable dream. Likewise, to describe the exact matter of the shift here would be as impossible as explaining the impact of a dream to someone who was not there dreaming it with you.

I will say this: I walked into my favorite coffee shop–bookstore that bright morning and took a seat at a table where someone had left a stack of books. On top was a slender volume titled *Caught in Fading Light*, and it had on its cover the dusky outline of a cougar. It told the story of the author, Gary Thorpe, tracking a mountain lion daily for over a year, and never seeing it.

Jung would call this synchronicity, two events connected by something stronger than chance. I didn't call it anything. If I'd been in another state of mind, it might have impressed me. Today, it just made sense. Just as it made sense that the next book in the stack was by Rainer Maria Rilke, and when I turned to the first page, my eyes fell on a poem in which Rilke, the poet, is struck silent by a sight so beautiful and unfathomable that it shifts his world. To him, it was an archaic statue of Apollo, an ancient god, an archetype. In the presence of the piece of art, Rilke sees everything that is possible in him, but which he has not yet become. He ends the poem with these lines:

Otherwise the shoulders
would not glisten like the fur of a wild animal:

would not, from all the borders of itself,
burst like pure light: for here there is no place
that does not see you. You must change your life.

Rilke, nearly a full century ago, called upon the image of a wild animal to illustrate that peaceful yet powerful strength that comes to us rarely and shifts our world. The possibility of it exists in all of us. It is the dream of a common mind that hearkens back through history, provides a connection between us all. Here, there is no place that does not see you.

I finished my drink, bought both books, and, well, as soon as I left the bookstore the mundane world wiggled its way back into my life. My cell phone rang. On the end of the line was a park ranger. "We have a report of a lion sighting in Chautauqua."

"Yes, I saw a lion."

"It stalked some teenagers?"

"It didn't stalk them. It walked behind them, looking for a place to go. It acted just like a lion should act. It was a good lion, a good lion." I knew that any behavior illustrating this cat had grown too accustomed to humans could label it a "bad cat" and put the animal at risk.

Though I knew that Kathleen had done the right thing by reporting my sighting (the cougar was on the tennis court, after all), it also felt somehow wrong to me.

Maybe my personal unconscious understood the need for monitoring a large predator's behavior, especially when people have chosen to live virtually in the predator's habitat. But at the same time, something in me, maybe my collective unconscious, wanted that cat to remain untouched by human eyes, uncontrolled by rangers, and completely wild.

The conversation I had with the ranger edged too close to an absurd moment I'd experienced in my little suburban home. I was out one morning at dawn, working in the garden, when a red fox emerged from the blonde, dried grasses in the open field behind my house. I stopped, leaned on my shovel, and fell momentarily in love with that fox. With its long, lean body, its bushy coat, the red that deepens to black on the tip of the tail—oh, yes, it really was love. Just then, a car pulled up to the stop sign on my corner. The woman in the car caught sight of the fox, too, and her jaw dropped. The window of her SUV was down, so I waved and called out to her, "Gorgeous, huh?" She picked up her cell phone and put it to her ear. I thought, *What an unfortunate time to receive a phone call, right when she could be taking in the sight of this magnificent fox running across the field at dawn.*

She looked frantic, though. So I picked up my shovel and walked closer to see if I could help. Close up, I saw she was indeed wan and frightened. "Did you see that animal?" she said.

"Yes." I kept up my bright smile.

She kept up her frenzied glare. "Good, good. Yes, I'm calling animal control right now," she said. Actually, she screamed it.

I wondered what this woman would do in the presence of a big cat. I wondered what she did in the presence of her Self. I wondered if it was different values that separated us, or different worlds. I wondered at the fear bubbling up so readily inside her, and at her trust in something—a phone call—that could so easily put that fear in check.

Luckily, my conversation with the ranger turned out to be nothing like my conversation with my neighbor. I had feared it might, until I realized, in true "Shadow form," that this ranger was doing exactly what I had done when I worked for the state parks. At the end of the conversation, she said, "Yeah, we know that lion, or at least we know of it. No one's seen it, but it has a kill over on the north side of the mountain. It was no doubt just heading out for its food."

Jung once said, "One does not become enlightened by imagining figures of light, but by making the darkness conscious."

If the lion, in all its dark, nocturnal otherness, in all its light, internal sameness, does not exist for future generations, if we destroy its habitat, or call open season on it, what could we possibly find to replace it? It is precisely because we fear large predators that we need them. They hold within them so many things we have lost, or are on the verge of losing, personally and collectively, permanently and forever. If we sacrifice the fear, we also sacrifice the strength, the wildness, the beauty, the awe.

In those few seconds when I was in the presence of the lion, I did not say to myself, *You must change your life.*

I knew, right then and there, that my life had been changed. A piece of something necessary had clicked into place inside me. I had become more aware, more intimate with my own fear and my own possibilities. I remembered what it was like to be humbled by awe. I became more compassionate. I became a better person.

DROUGHT

Oregon — A river's dying off reveals what is at stake for the natural world that depends on it and the extent one man will go to bring it back to life. For this author, it is the powerful metaphor of cougar that indicates the return of wildness and what humankind and nature need to survive.

I awoke one night and thought I heard rain—it was the dry needles of fir trees falling on the roof. Men with an intolerable air of condolence have appeared, as though drawn by the smell of death, dressed comfortably, speaking in a manipulated tongue, terminally evil. They have inquired into the purchase of our homes. And reporters come and go, outraged over the absence of brown trout, which have never been here. The river like some great whale lies dying in the forest.

In the years we have been here I have trained myself to listen to the river, not in the belief that I could understand what it said, but only from one day to the next know its fate. The river's language arose principally from two facts: the slightest change in its depth brought it into contact with a different portion of the stones along its edges and the rocks and boulders midstream that lay in its way, and so changed its tone; and although its movement around one object may seem uniform at any one time it is in fact changeable.

167

Added to these major variations are the landings of innumerable insects on its surface, the breaking of its waters by fish, the falling into it of leaves and twigs, the slooshing of raccoons, the footfalls of deer; ultimately these are the only commentary on the river's endless reading of the surface of the earth over which it flows.

It was in this way that I learned before anyone else of the coming drought. Day after day as the river fell by imperceptible increments its song changed, notes came that were unknown to me. I mentioned this to no one, but each morning when I awoke I went immediately to the river's edge and listened. It was as though I could hear the sound rain begins to make in a country where it is not going to come for a long time.

As the water fell, however, nothing unexpected was uncovered, although the effect of standing in areas once buried beneath the roar of the river's current was unsettling. I found only one made object, a wheel, the kind you find on the back of a child's tricycle. But I didn't look as closely as the others. The wailing of the river over its last stones was difficult to bear, yet it was this that drew me back each day, as one visits those dying hopelessly in a hospital room. During those few hours each morning I would catch stranded fish barehanded in shallow pools and release them where the river still flowed. The bleaching of algae once waving green underwater to white; river stones once cool now hot to the touch and dry; spider webs stretched where there had been salmon eggs; snakes where there had been trout—it was as though the river had been abandoned.

During those summer days, absorbed with the death of the river and irritated at the irreverent humor of weather forecasters in distant cities, I retreated into a state of isolation. I fasted and abstained as much as I felt appropriate from water. These were only gestures, of course, but even as a boy I knew a gesture might mean life or death and I believed the universe was similarly triggered.

From this point on, the song that came out of the river did not bother me as much. I sat out of the way of the pounding sun, in dark rocks shaded by the overhanging branches of alders along the bank. Their dry leaves, stirred by the breeze, fell brittle and pale around me. I slept on the bank regularly now. I would say very simple prayers in the evening, only an expression of camaraderie, stretching my fingers gently into the darkness toward the inchoate source of the river's strangulation. I did not beg. There was a power to dying, and it should be done with grace. I was only making a gesture on the shore, a speck in the steep, brutal dryness of the valley by a dying river.

In moments of great depression, of an unfathomable compassion in myself, I would make the agonized and tentative movements of a dance, like a long-legged bird. I would exhort the river.

What death we saw. Garter snake stiff as a twig in the rocks. Trees (young ones, too young) crying out in the night, shuddering, dropping all their leaves. Farther from the river, birds falling dead in thickets, animals dead on their paths, their hands stiffened in gestures of bewilderment and beseeching; the color gone out of the eyes of any creature you met, for whom, out of respect, you would step off the path to allow to pass.

Where a trickle of water still flowed there was an atmosphere of truce, more dangerous than one might imagine. As deer and coyote slipped from the same tiny pool they abrogated their agreement, and the deer contemplated the loss of the coyote as he would the loss of a friend; for the enemy, like the friend, made you strong. I was alert for such moments, for they were augury, but I was wary of them as of any lesson learned in death.

One moonlit evening I dreamed of a certain fish. The fish was gray-green against light-colored stones at the bottom of a deep pool, breathing a slow, unperturbed breath, the largest fish I had ever imagined living in the river. The sparkling of the water around him and the sound of it cascading over the creek bed made me weak and I awoke suddenly, convulsed. I knew the fish. I knew the place. I set out immediately.

The dry riverbed was only a clattering of teetering stones now, ricocheting off my feet as I passed, bone-weary, feeling disarmed by hunger, by the dimness of the night, and by the irrefutable wisdom and utter foolishness of what I was doing. As I drew near the mouth of the creek the fish began to loom larger and larger and I could feel—as though my hands were extended to a piece of cloth flapping in the darkness—both the hope and futility of such acts.

I found the spot where the creek came in and went up it. I had seen the fish once in a deep pool below a rapids where he had fed himself too well and grown too large to escape. There was a flow of night air coming down the creek bed, rattling dry leaves. In the faint moonlight a thousand harlequin beetles suddenly settled on my clothing and I knew how close I was to a loss of conviction, to rage, to hurling what beliefs I had like a handful of pebbles into the bushes.

The beetles clung to the cloth, moved through my hair, came into the cups of my hands as I walked, and as suddenly were gone, and the area I stood in was familiar, the fish before me. The rapids were gone. The pool had become a pit. In its lowest depression the huge fish lay motionless, but for the faint lifting of a gill cover. I climbed down to him and wrapped him in my shirt, soaked in the pool. I had expected, I think, a fight, to be punched in that pit by the fish who lay in my arms now like a cold lung.

Climbing out of there, stopping wherever I could to put his head under some miserable pool, hurrying, I came to the river and the last trickle of water, where I released him without ceremony.

I knew, as I had known in the dream, the danger I was in but I knew, too, that without such an act of self-assertion no act of humility had meaning.

By now the river was only a whisper. I stood at the indistinct edge and exhorted what lay beyond the river, which now seemed more real than the river itself. With no more strength than there is in a bundle of sticks I tried to dance, to dance the dance of the long-legged birds who lived in the shallows. I danced it because I could not think of anything more beautiful.

The turning came during the first days of winter. Lynx came down from the north to what was left of the river. Deer were with him. And from some other direction Raccoon and Porcupine. And from downriver Weasel and White-footed Mouse, and from above Blue Heron and Goshawk. Badger came up out of the ground with

Mole. They stood near me in staring silence and I was afraid to move. Finally Blue Heron spoke: "We were the first people here. We gave away all the ways of living. Now no one remembers how to live anymore, so the river is drying up. Before we could ask for rain there had to be someone to do something completely selfless, with no hope of success. You went after that fish, and then at the end, you were trying to dance. A person cannot be afraid of being foolish. For everything, every gesture, is sacred.

"Now, stand up and learn this dance. It is going to rain."

We danced together on the bank. And the songs we danced to were river songs I remembered from long ago. We danced until I could not understand the words but only the sounds, and the sounds were unmistakably the sound rain makes when it is getting ready to come into a country.

I awoke in harsh light one morning, moved back into the trees and fell asleep again. I awoke later to what I thought were fir needles falling on my cheeks but these were drops of rain.

It rained for weeks. Not hard, but steadily. The river came back easily. There were no floods. People said it was a blessing. They offered explanations enough. Backs were clapped, reputations lost and made, the seeds of future argument and betrayal sown, wounds suffered and allowed, pride displayed. It was no different from any other birth but for a lack of joy and, for that, stranger than anything you can imagine, inhuman and presumptuous. But people go their way, and with reason; and the hardness for some is all but unfathomable, and so begs forgiveness. Everyone has to learn how to die, that song, that dance, alone and in time.

The river has come back to fit between the banks. To stick your hands into the river is to feel the cords that bind the earth together in one piece. The sound of it at a distance is like wild horses in a canyon, going sure-footed away from the smell of a cougar come to them faintly on the wind.

COUGAR COUNTRY SAFETY TIPS

SAFETY TIPS

By nature, mountain lions are elusive and reclusive, preferring to avoid contact with humans at all costs. In fact, upon seeing a human, cougars usually run. At the same time, cougars have a curiosity not unlike that of housecats. The possibility of triggering this curiosity should reinforce the necessity of taking caution when living or recreating in cougar country. Understanding the behavior of mountain lions can greatly minimize the potential of coming into contact with one of nature's keystone species.

Cougar attacks are extremely rare. Since 1890, only twenty people have died or been killed as a result of an attack. Although these deaths are tragic, National Safety Council statistics show that there are many other things we encounter on a daily basis that are much more likely to lead to fatalities. For example, compare the eighteen cougar-related deaths over the last 100 years to the eighteen people who died from dog bites in 2002 alone. Even more common are car accidents. In 2002, there were 48,366 transportation-related deaths.

Although the statistics reinforce how unlikely cougar attacks are, we recognize that some people live or recreate in habitat where encounters may be more likely. Fears can be eased with a better understanding of these environments. Most urbanites lock their doors to protect themselves and their property, to avoid the risks associated with the urban environment within which they live. Similarly, if you are going to buy or build a home or recreate in a place where cougars and other wild animals live, you need to learn about their behavior and habits and learn how to act responsibly in this environment. Following are some suggested tips for living and recreating in cougar country.

GUIDELINES FOR LIVING IN COUGAR COUNTRY

- Be aware of your surroundings. Contact your state game agency and learn about the wildlife in your area. Talk to your neighbors.

- Cougars' most active hours are during dawn and dusk. Consider this fact when gardening, letting your dog or cat out, or being outdoors.

- Install outside lighting. Motion-activated lights placed where you walk are particularly helpful.

- Supervise children. Educate them about wildlife and how to behave if they encounter a cougar.

- Landscape wisely. Deer-proof your yard, using netting or maintaining a garden that does not attract deer or other prey. Prune dense vegetation, which cougars may use for cover. Remember that if you live in or near cougar country, where there are deer, there could be a cougar.

- Consider the consequences of feeding wildlife, including birds. In some places, birdseed will attract animals that cougars may prey upon.

- Keep pets secure. Roaming pets are easy prey. Do not leave their food outside as it may attract raccoons or other animals. Again, cougars follow prey. Store all garbage securely.

- Protect, fence, and shelter livestock and hobby animals. Place in enclosed sheds or barns at night.

GUIDELINES FOR RECREATING IN COUGAR COUNTRY

- Learn about the places and wildlife living where you hike, bike, ski, or climb. Be especially alert when recreating at dawn or dusk, peak times for cougars.

- Consider recreating with others. When in groups, you are less likely to surprise a cougar. If alone, consider carrying bear spray or attaching a bell to yourself or your backpack. Tell a friend where you are going and when you plan to return.

- Supervise children and pets. Keep them close to you. Teach children about cougars and how to recreate responsibly. Instruct them about how to behave in the event of an encounter.

- If you come into contact with a cougar that does not run away, stay calm, stand your ground, and don't back down! Back away slowly if possible and safe to do so. Pick up children, but DO NOT BEND DOWN or turn your back on the cougar. DO NOT RUN. Running triggers an innate response in cougars that could lead to an attack.

- Raise your voice and speak firmly. Raise your arms to make yourself look larger, clap your hands, and throw something you might have in your hands, like a water bottle. Again, do not bend over to pick up a stone off the ground. This action may trigger a pounce response in a cougar.

- If in the very unusual event that a cougar attacks you, fight back. People have successfully fought off cougars with rocks, sticks, garden tools, etc. Try to remain standing and get up if you fall to the ground.

- If you believe an encounter to be a valid public safety concern, contact your state game agency and any local wildlife organizations.

DEATHS BY COUGAR ATTACK,
1890–PRESENT

The following is based on criteria developed by Professor of Conservation Biology and Wildlife Ecology Paul Beier, School of Forestry, Northern Arizona University, in documenting cougarcaused human deaths. Included within these parameters are attacks that led to death as reported by verifiable sources, such as newspapers, medical records, statements of wildlife personnel, and reports of state or provincial wildlife management agencies where the attacks occurred.

Deaths by Cougar Attack, 1890–Present

When	Where	Who/Description
June 19, 1890	Quartz Valley, Siski County, California, USA	**7-year-old boy, Arthur Dangle** Arthur was killed by two lions while playing among oak trees some distance from his home.
July 5, 1909	Morgan Hill in Santa Clara County, California, USA	**38-year-old woman, Isola Kennedy, and 10-year-old boy, Earl Wilson** A mountain lion injured Isola Kennedy and Earl Wilson near Morgan Hill in Santa Clara County. Isola and Earl were said to have died of rabies nine weeks and seven weeks later, respectively, but no tests were done, and they more likely died of blood poisoning as the symptoms of high fever, lockjaw, and spinal meningitis were listed. According to the June 1994 Animal People Online News, "Jogger's death starts puma panic: Morgan Hill school teacher Isola Kennedy, thirty-eight, and her pupil Earl Wilson, eight, survived their wounds, but died of the rabies or blood poisoning some weeks later."
December 17, 1924	Olema, Washington, USA	**13-year-old boy, Jimmie Fehlhaber** Jimmie had been sent to pick up a team of horses at a neighboring ranch. On snowshoes, he took a shortcut that followed a winding trail and dropped down into a coulee at one point. Tracks in the snow indicated the cat had followed the boy, staying out of sight in the brush to one side of the trail. When Jimmie finally spotted the cat, he ran to a small tree, probably with the hope of climbing it. He managed to cover 100 yards before the cougar leapt onto him and knocked him to the ground. Evidence showed that the boy fought back, stabbing and slashing the cougar with a small jackknife. But the cougar prevailed. The boy's hands were badly chewed up and his thigh partially consumed before the cougar partially covered his body and left. Recovered at the scene were the open jackknife, a good-luck charm the boy carried, and the animal's left front dewclaw, which

continued on next page

Deaths by Cougar Attack, 1890–Present – *continued*

When	Where	Who/Description
December 17, 1924	Olema, Washington, USA	(13-year-old boy, Jimmie Fehlhaber – *continued*) he had managed to cut off before he died. A bounty was offered and the cougar was shot. Accounts of the animal vary widely: some reported the cougar to be in good health whereas another described him as in a state of starvation; its age was given by some as three years old and by others as thirteen years old; one reported a male, another a female. Even the number of cougars involved is confused: one report states that two cats were responsible, and another just one.
June 1, 1949	150 km north of Tofino, British Columbia, CANADA	7-year-old boy, Dominic Taylor The boy was mauled and dragged into the bush while walking on the beach. The cougar was scared off by the boy's father, who heard his son's cries for help, but it was too late.
January 3, 1971	Lytton, British Columbia, CANADA	12-year-old boy, Lawrence Wells Lawrence was mauled to death by a twelve-year-old male cougar near Lytton, British Columbia, while playing near his home with his two younger sisters. His father shot the cougar, but the boy was already dead.
January 20, 1974	Arroyo Seco, New Mexico, USA	8-year-old boy, Kenneth Clark Nolan Kenneth was killed by a forty-seven-pound, emaciated, three-year-old female cougar. Kenneth was playing in the rabbit brush and gullies with his seven-year-old half brother David Cordry less than a mile from their home. Suddenly they glanced up and saw a mountain lion ready to pounce; the cougar caught Kenneth and started biting him on the back. David tried to push the lion away, and it reached for him with its forepaws, tearing the boy's coat and inflicting superficial scratches. David then ran for help but was so hysterical that it took him twenty minutes to direct his father, state patrolman David Cordry, to the attack site. Their German shepherd-mix dog began baying, which led them to the

cougar standing over the dead boy. Cordry shot the lion with his revolver three times before the still-snarling lion fled. His neighbor James Meyer took up the chase and killed the wounded cougar with his rifle. Although emaciated and having insufficient white blood cells, possibly due to severe infection or a fatal condition, the animal was found to be not rabid. The necropsy report was inconclusive as to whether this cat had ever been a pet or captive.

| July 14, 1976 | Gold River, British Columbia on Vancouver Island, CANADA | **7-year-old girl, Matilda May Samuel** |

Matilda May Samuel of Port Alberni was killed by a two-year-old male cougar while picking berries along a gravel road near Gold River, British Columbia. She was with an adult and an older child. (Etling reports that she was with a fifteen-year-old girl and seventeen-year-old boy.) When they heard the noise and saw the cougar already upon Matilda, they shouted at it and the cougar backed away, but only briefly. Then it pounced on Matilda again. At that point, the police said, the two were too frightened to do anything but run for help. Matilda was visiting relatives who lived on a nearby Indian reserve across the road from the Muchalat pulp mill, where many local people worked. Unknown to the three, just a few hours earlier, a cougar had stalked a mill worker and then given serious chase to him as he drove away on his motorcycle that he was riding to work at the mill. The man did not report this until after hearing of Matilda's death. The cougar also had been eating from the carcass of a recently killed deer. The cougar still had fresh remains from a deer kill in its stomach.

| May 16, 1988 | Tofino, British Columbia, CANADA | **9-year-old boy, Jesse Sky Bergman** |

Jesse Sky Bergman was killed by a four-year-old male cougar near Tofino, British Columbia. He had gone to visit his father about five miles north of Tofino. His body was found badly mauled about the head. Paw prints indicated the cat had stalked him.

continued on next page

Deaths by Cougar Attack, 1890–Present – *continued*

When	Where	Who/Description
September 9, 1989	Evaro, Missoula County, Montana, USA	**5-year-old boy, Jake Thomas Gardipee** At least two and possibly three mountain lions attacked and killed Jake of Missoula County (Evaro), Montana, while he was riding a tricycle behind his home. Trapper Francis Cahoon said Jake could have been killed by a female lion traveling with cubs or by a pair of yearling siblings. Searchers scared off an adult mountain lion when they found the boy's body. Another fifty-two-pound yearling with blood on its paws and mouth was killed 100 yards away. Cahoon said that all they knew is that the cat killed was not the only cat that attacked Jake.
January 14, 1991	Idaho Springs, Colorado, USA	**18-year-old boy, Scott Lancaster** Scott Lancaster was killed while jogging at his high school track in Idaho Springs, Colorado. The youth was attacked by a mountain lion and dragged 200 yards uphill before being killed. The 130-pound boy clutched at vegetation and uprooted brush as the lion dragged him to the killing ground. Although just a few hundred yards from high school, Scott's screams for help went unheard. The lion was found three days later, still feeding on the boy. Lancaster was buried following a closed casket ceremony. This was the first death ever in Colorado from a lion attack.
March 10, 1991	La Quinta, California, USA	**3-year-old boy, Travis Zweig** Travis Zweig of La Quinta, California, was feared killed by a mountain lion after he wandered away from his father, who was chopping wood at a remote cabin near Piñon Pines, California. Searchers combing rugged terrain for the boy found evidence suggesting a mountain lion dragged him off, authorities say. Shoe prints thought to be the toddler's were found a half-mile from where Travis disappeared. Sheriff's sergeant Craig Kilday said the prints stopped at a rocky overhang where mountain lion prints were found. Where the shoe prints stopped, there was a slide area and what they believed to be drag marks. This would be the first fatality from a mountain lion attack in California

since a boy was killed in 1890, according to the Orange County Cooperative Mountain Lion Study, and only a dozen such fatal attacks had taken place since 1890 in all of North America at the time of Travis's disappearance.

May 1992	Kyuquot, British Columbia, CANADA	**7-year-old boy, Jeremy Williams** Jeremy Williams of Kyuquot, British Columbia, was mauled to death by a yearling female cougar as he played on the edge of the school yard. Jeremy, a Kyuquot Indian boy, was attacked as he sat on the grass in the elementary school playground. The cougar rushed and attacked the freckled, red-haired youngster. The boy's father and a dozen youngsters witnessed the attack. Kevin Williams, Jeremy's father and a teacher at the school, hurried to the scene and watched helplessly while children screamed in panic. The school's janitor shot and killed the sixty-pound lion. Richard Leo, a Kyuquot Indian chief, said angry parents accused the school board of ignoring the danger of wild animals.
December 10, 1994	Cuyamaca Rancho State Park, California, USA	**56-year-old woman, Iris M. Kenna** Iris M. Kenna, at five feet, four inches tall and weighing no more than 115 pounds, was in excellent physical condition when she was killed near Cuyamaca Peak at Cuyamaca Rancho State Park, California, while hiking to Cuyamaca Peak alone in the early morning. She was attacked near the bench dedicated to her at the intersection of the Lookout Fire Road and Azalea Springs Fire Road / Fern Flat Fire Road.
August 19, 1996	Princeton, British Columbia, CANADA	**35- or 36-year-old woman, Cindy Parolin** Cindy Parolin and three of her four children were trail riding on horseback near Princeton, British Columbia, when their horses became increasingly nervous. A mountain lion suddenly jumped from a bush at the six-year-old son. The boy was thrown from his horse and was attacked by the mountain lion. The mother leapt from her horse and clubbed the lion away from her son with a branch she was able to break off a nearby tree. Then she continued to fight the animal and instructed her two other children to drag the injured youngster to the safety of their car and then get help. Finally, her older son found

continued on next page

Deaths by Cougar Attack, 1890–Present – *continued*

When	Where	Who/Description
August 19, 1996	Princeton, British Columbia, CANADA	**(35- or 36-year-old woman, Cindy Parolin** – *continued*) an armed camper, Jim Manion, who was led to the scene. He found Cindy still fighting more than an hour later. Much of her upper torso had been consumed. She asked if her children were okay, and when Jim said yes, she said in a half-whisper, "I am dying now," and she collapsed. Jim fired a shot to scare the lion away and then hit the lion and it fled into the brush. Wildlife officials later found it where it had died about 150 feet from the trail. Cindy died from her injuries. Her son Steven, who had been attacked, survived. The male mountain lion weighed only sixty-five pounds.
July 17, 1997	Rocky Mountain National Park, Colorado, USA	**10-year-old boy, Mark Miedema** A boy from Lakewood, Mark Miedema, was killed by an adult female cougar about 4:30 P.M. during a hike in Rocky Mountain National Park. He had raced ahead of his family on a well-traveled trail and was out of sight. His family arrived to see his feet and legs extending onto the trail from adjacent brush. The cougar attempted to drag him away before fleeing. Mark died from choking on his own vomit. The lion retreated when the parents arrived but was killed soon afterward when it tried to pounce on a National Park Service officer who was guarding the boy's body. This is the second death ever in Colorado from a lion attack; two other hikers were attacked by cougars in Colorado in the previous year.
October 2, 1999	Larimer County, Colorado, USA	**3-year-old boy, Jaryd John Atadero** Evidence uncovered in June 2003 positively indicates that Jaryd was killed and carried away by a mountain lion. From the initial 1999 investigations, officials had theorized that Jaryd may have been attacked and dragged off by a mountain lion. There were multiple reports of cougar signs and sightings in the area. Until three years and eight months after his disappearance, however, no trace of him had been found in the area where he had been hiking in Poudre Canyon, Colorado. Hiding and trying to scare his companions

along the trail, he had become separated from his sister and eleven adults, themselves separated into two groups. Tragically, two fishermen he encountered around noon neglected to restrain the wandering child when he had asked them where he could find bears. On June 4, 2003, Jaryd's clothing was found by hikers on a rock slope 436 feet above the trail where the boy was hiking when he disappeared northwest of Fort Collins. After an official search was begun, his remains (a molar and the top of his skull) were found ten days later about 150 feet from where his clothing was discovered.

January 2, 2001	**Banff National Park, Alberta, CANADA**

30-year-old woman, Frances Frost

Frances Frost, a cross-country skier, was killed by a mountain lion in Banff National Park while skiing alone around 1:00 P.M. on Cascade Fire Road, part of the Lake Minnewanka Loop. According to park chief warden Ian Syme, the cougar, which was more than six feet long, stalked Frost by hiding behind a tree at some distance from the trail. As she passed by, heading toward the trailhead, the animal bounded up behind her, jumped on her back, bit her neck, and killed her. "I suspect that she may not even know what hit her." A healthy adult male cougar (eight years old) was later shot by wardens where it was found standing over her body. Reports did not say if Frances had been consumed. This is the first death by cougar in the history of the park and in Alberta. Park wardens think that elk, the main prey of wolves and cougars, have moved closer to Banff because hunting is not allowed in national parks, and the cougars and wolves have followed.

May 3, 2003	**Leslie, Arkansas, USA**

41-year-old woman, Leigh Ann Cox

Probably at about 5:00 P.M. Leigh Ann Cox was killed by a large cat near Leslie, Arkansas. Details of this incident are still unresolved. At 9:57 P.M., Morton, an EMT, responded to the call by Leigh's brother-in-law, Ken Davison, and sister. When Morton got to the remote Davison residence, Ken, an ex-police officer, had shot two of his five dogs, believing they were the only possible explanation for her death, as wildlife officials had insisted over and over to many individuals in the Chimes area that despite numerous reports of

continued on next page

Deaths by Cougar Attack, 1890–Present — continued

When	Where	Who/Description
May 3, 2003	Leslie, Arkansas, USA	**(41-year-old woman, Leigh Cox** — *continued)* sightings, no cougars were in Arkansas. Morton recognized what he believed were the signs of cat involvement within seconds of examining Leigh Ann's body. Leigh Ann's scalp had been ripped off, apparently from the front to the back, almost in one piece from her forehead to the nape of her neck. She had slash marks identified as typical of a large cat but impossible for a dog to make. Morton also thought her neck was broken and her trachea probably crushed from the angulation of the neck, indicating a sudden death. Morton convinced Davison to cease shooting his dogs.
January 8, 2004	Whiting Ranch Wilderness Park in Orange County, California, USA	**35-year-old man, Mark Jeffrey Reynolds** Approximately between noon and 2:00 P.M., Mark Jeffrey Reynolds, of adjoining Foothill Ranch, California, a five-foot, nine-inch, 135-pound competitive mountain bike racer, was killed by a mountain lion while biking on a section of trail known as Cactus Ridge Run at Whiting Ranch Wilderness Park in southern Orange County. His bicycle was later found with the chain broken off. Jim Amormino, a spokesman for the Orange County Sheriff's Department, speculated that Reynolds was attacked as he was fixing his bike. When another cyclist, Nils Magnuson, first found Reynolds's bicycle, he was about to look for Reynolds but was interrupted by the women's screams, those of two other mountain bikers, Anne Hjelle and her friend Debi Nichols, on the trail. Hjelle had been jumped by the same cougar, and Nichols was successful in fighting the cat off. (Mountain bikers crash fairly frequently, so finding a crashed bicycle is not an unusual occurrence. It is customary to stop and render aid to crashees.) After the attack on Anne Hjelle, Reynolds's body was spotted by the rescue helicopter crew higher on the trail than where Hjelle was attacked. Reynolds had apparently been dead for a few hours, and his body had been half-eaten and partially buried, typical of a mountain lion kill.

COUGARS KILLED BY HUMANS,
1900–2000

       The below chart represents the cumu-
lative number of cougars killed in eleven western states over the
course of a century. Individual states' cougar kill numbers vary
and fall within the range depicted below. (Note: Following the
period of persecution, game agencies assigned official hunt seasons
to restrict the numbers of cougars that could be killed. In spite of
this, the killing of cougars has increased four to five times since
these "protections" were implemented in the late 1960s.)

COUGAR MORTALITY

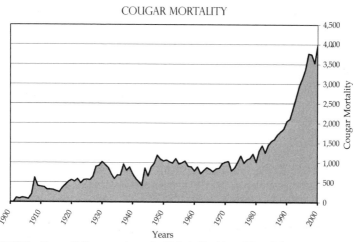

Years

© 2007 by Steven G. Torres, redrawn by Rick A. Hopkins of Live Oak Associates, Inc.

Mapping Values: Cougars and the Perspectives of Human Stakeholders

This map summarizes the vast interests of people involved in and affected by cougar conservation, management, and activism. It was researched, written and compiled by David Mattson, Wildlife Researcher, USGS , and Susan G. Clark, Ph.D., Wildlife Ecologist and Policy Scientist at Yale University.

Participant	Identities	Nature-Views	Material Stakes	Value Stakes
Livestock producers	Rural; politically conservative	Dominionistic Utilitarian Negativistic	Depredation losses	Skill, achieveme Security, traditi Wealth
Ungulate hunters	Caucasian males Non-metropolitan Outdoor active Attracted to wildlife Knowledgeable of wildlife Politically conservative	Dominionistic Utilitarian Naturalistic Ecologistic	Huntable ungulates	Skill, achieveme Power
Cougar hunters	Caucasian males Non-metropolitan Outdoor active Attracted to wildlife Knowledgeable of wildlife Politically conservative	Dominionistic Utilitarian Naturalistic Ecologistic	Huntable cougars	Skill, achieveme Power Wealth
Wildlife agency commis- sioners	Caucasian males Non-metropolitan Outdoor active Attracted to wildlife Knowledgeable of wildlife	Dominionistic Utilitarian Naturalistic Ecologistic	Huntable ungulates Agency budgets	Power Skill, achieveme Wealth
Wildlife agency personnel	Caucasian males Non-metropolitan Outdoor active Attracted to wildlife Knowledgeable of wildlife	Naturalistic Ecologistic Dominionistic Utilitarian	Huntable wildlife Agency budgets	Skill, achieveme Power Wealth Enlightenment

Claims & Beliefs	Demands & Preferences
Local knowledge & lifeways should have primacy Depredation losses are unacceptable	Compensate & prevent depredation Reduce or eliminate cougars
North American conservation ethic Scientific management Hunting is necessary & ethical Hunting instills fear, reduces conflict, & is good for cougars	Hunt cougars with hounds Resolve conflicts lethally Reduce cougar populations to benefit ungulates & increase hunting opportunities
Hunting cougars with hounds is logical & ethical Hound hunting instills fear, reduces conflicts, & removes large males to benefit other cougars	Hunt cougars with hounds Resolve conflicts lethally Maintain cougar hunting opportunities
North American conservation ethic Scientific management Total quality management Hunting is necessary & ethical Hunting instills fear & reduces conflicts Conflict can be resolved thru education	Hunt cougars with hounds Resolve conflicts lethally Reduce cougar populations to benefit ungulates, increase hunting opportunities, & reduce depredation
North American conservation ethic Scientific management Total quality management Hunting is necessary & ethical Hunting instills fear & reduces conflicts Conflict can be resolved thru education	Hunt cougars with hounds Resolve conflicts lethally Reduce cougar populations to benefit ungulates, increase hunting opportunities, & reduce depredation

continued on next page

Mapping Values: Cougars and the Perspectives of Human Stakeholders — *continued*

Participant	Identities	Nature-Views	Material Stakes	Value Stakes
"The public"	Caucasian male heads of household	Ecologistic	—	—
Animal-focused activists	Caucasian females Urban Well educated Politically liberal	Humanistic Moralistic Naturalistic Ecologistic	Live cougars Ecologically functional cougar populations	Rectitude
Environ-mentalists	Caucasian Politically liberal	Ecologistic Naturalistic Moralistic Humanistic	Wilderness Ecologically functional cougar populations	Rectitude

Claims & Beliefs	Demands & Preferences
Cougars have important ecological role Cougars are not a major threat Endangering kittens and hunting with hounds are unethical	Kill cougars that have injured or killed humans, to protect endangered and threatened species, and to protect children Do not kill cougars to increase hunting opportunities Prohibit hunting with hounds
Hunting is unethical Endangering kittens and hunting with hounds is unethical Cougars have important ecological role Hunting does not reduce conflicts Humans responsible for living with cougars	Prohibit cougar hunting Prohibit hunting females & hunting with hounds Maintain ecologically functional cougar populations
Cougars have important ecological role Endangering kittens and hunting with hounds are unethical Hunting does not reduce conflicts	Humans responsible for living with cougars Prohibit hunting females & hunting with hounds Maintain ecologically functional cougar populations

ORGANIZATIONS AND
RELATED WEB SITES

Animal Protection of New Mexico: www.apnm.org
Beringia South: www.beringiasouth.org
Boone and Crockett Club: www.boone-crockett.org
Conservation International: www.conservationinternational.org
Cougar Fund: www.cougarfund.org
Craighead Environmental Research Institute: www.craigheadresearch.org
Eastern Cougar Network: www.easterncougarnet.org
Foundation for North American Wild Sheep: www.fnaws.org
Humane Society of the United States: www.hsus.org
Jane Goodall Institute: www.janegoodall.org
Mountain Lion Foundation: www.mountainlion.org
Nature Conservancy: www.nature.org
Northern Rockies Conservation Cooperative: www.nrccooperative.org
People for the Ethical Treatment of Animals: www.peta.org
Rocky Mountain Elk Foundation: www.rmef.org
Roots and Shoots: www.rootsandshoots.org
Safari Club International: www.safariclub.org
Sinapu: www.sinapu.org
Sportsmen for Fish and Wildlife: www.sfwsfh.org
Western Association of Fish and Wildlife Agencies: www.wafwa.org
Wildlife Conservation Society: www.wcs.org

FOR FURTHER READING

Bekoff, Marc. *Animal Passions and Beastly Virtues: Reflections on Redecorating Nature*. Philadelphia: Temple University Press, 2005.

Bekoff, Marc. *The Emotional Lives of Animals*. New York: HarperCollins Books, 2006.

Blessley, Cara Shea. *Spirit of the Rockies: The Mountain Lions of Jackson Hole*, with photos by Tom Mangelsen. Omaha, NE: Images of Nature, 2000.

Bolgiano, Chris. *Mountain Lion: An Unnatural History of Pumas and People*. Mechanicsburg, PA: Stackpole Books, 1995.

Bolgiano, Chris, and Jerry Roberts. *The Eastern Cougar: Historic Accounts, Scientific Investigations, and New Evidence*. Mechanicsburg, PA: Stackpole Books, 2005.

Busch, Robert H. *The Cougar Almanac: A Complete Natural History of the Mountain Lion*. Guilford, CT: Lyons Press, 2004.

Clark, Timothy W., A. Peyton Curlee, Steven C. Minta, and Peter Kareiva. *Carnivores in Ecosystems: The Yellowstone Experience*. New Haven, CT: Yale University Press, 1999.

Cougar Management Guidelines Working Group. *Cougar Management Guidelines*. Salem, OR: Sharon Negri/Opal Creek Press, 2005.

Danz, Harold P. *Cougar*. Athens, OH: Swallow Press / Ohio University Press, 1999.

Ewing, Susan, and Elizabeth Grossman. *Shadow Cat: Encountering the American Mountain Lion*. Seattle: Sasquatch Books, 1999.

Fascione, Nina, Aimee Delach, and Martin Smith, eds. *People and Predators: From Conflict to Coexistence*. Washington, DC: Island Press, 2004.

Gittleman, John L., Stephen M. Funk, David W. MacDonald, and Robert K. Wayne, eds. *Carnivore Conservation*. Cambridge, England: Cambridge University Press, 2003.

Hansen, Kevin. *Cougar: The American Lion*. Flagstaff, AZ: Northland Press, 1992.

Hornocker, Maurice, and Sharon Negri. *Cougar Ecology and Conservation*. Chicago: University of Chicago Press, forthcoming 2008.

Leopold, Aldo. *A Sand County Almanac*. Oxford, England: Oxford University Press, 1949.

Logan, Kenneth A., and Linda L. Sweanor. *Desert Puma: Evolutionary Ecology and Conservation of an Enduring Carnivore*. Washington, DC: Island Press, 2001.

Ray, Justina, Kent Redford, Robert Steneck, and Joel Berger, eds. *Large Carnivores and the Conservation of Biodiversity*. Washington, DC: Island Press, 2005.

Shaw, Harley. *Soul Among Lions: The Cougar as Peaceful Adversary*. Tucson: University of Arizona Press, 2000.

Shepard, Paul. *The Tender Carnivore and the Sacred Game*. Athens: University of Georgia Press, 1973.

Thomas, Elizabeth Marshall. *The Tribe of Tiger: Cats and Their Culture*. New York: Simon & Schuster, 1994.

Torres, Steve. *The Mountain Lion Alert: Safety for Outdoor Adventurers and Landowners*. Guilford, CT: Falcon Press, 1997.

Turner, Jack. *The Abstract Wild*. Tucson: University of Arizona Press, 1996.

Woodroffe, Rosie, Simon Thurgood, and Alan Rabinowitz, eds. *People and Wildlife: Conflict or Co-existence?* Cambridge, England: Cambridge University Press, 2005.

BIOGRAPHICAL NOTES

RICK BASS's works are concerned with the nature of the human heart and the heart of nature. The son of a geologist, Bass took an early interest in the natural world. Bass published his first novel, *Where the Sea Used to Be,* in 1998. His most recent fictional works are a short story collection titled *The Hermit's Story: Stories* (Mariner Books, 2002) and *The Diezmo: A Novel* (Houghton Mifflin, 2005). Most of his other recent works have been nonfiction, including *The Ninemile Wolves* (Mariner Books, 1998), *Brown Dog of the Yaak: Essays on Art and Activism* (1999), *Colter: The True Story of the Best Dog I Ever Had* (Mariner Books, 2000), and *The Roadless Yaak: Reflections and Observations About One of Our Last Great Wilderness Areas* (The Lyons Press, 2003).

MARC BEKOFF is professor emeritus of Ecology and Evolutionary Biology at the University of Colorado, Boulder, a fellow of the Animal Behavior Society, and a former Guggenheim Fellow. In 2000 he was given the Exemplar Award from the Animal Behavior Society for major long-term contributions to the field of animal behavior. He and Jane Goodall cofounded the organization Ethologists for the Ethical Treatment of Animals in 2000.

Marc has published more than 200 papers and 20 books, including *Minding Animals: Awareness, Emotions, and Heart* (Oxford University Press, 2002), *The Ten Trusts: What We Must Do to Care For the Animals We Love*, with Jane Goodall (HarperCollins, 2002), *The Emotional Lives of Animals: A Leading Scientist Explores Animal Joy, Sorrow, and Empathy — and Why They Matter* (New World Library, 2007), and *Animals Matter* (Shambhala Publications, 2007). He has also edited a three-volume *Encyclopedia of Animal Behavior* (Greenwood Publishing, 2004) and a four-volume *Encyclopedia of Human-Animal Relationships* (Greenwood Publishing, 2007). In 2005, Marc was presented with The Bank One Faculty Community Service Award for the work he has done with children, senior citizens, and prisoners. Marc travels the world, speaking on behalf of animals. His homepage is http://literati.net/Bekoff.

JANAY BRUN has been conducting her own puma research concerning the use of grasslands by pumas on the Buenos Aires Wildlife Refuge, located in Sasabe, Arizona. She currently resides in Arivaca, Arizona, which is about a dozen miles from the border with Mexico.

JULIA B. CORBETT is an associate professor in the Department of Communication at the University of Utah. Her book *Communicating Nature: How We Create and Understand Environmental Messages* was published in 2006 by Island Press.

DEANNA DAWN is a wildlife biologist living in San Jose, California. Her interest in cougars began with her graduate work, which focused on cougar management in the United States. Deanna has conducted field research on cougars in California, Idaho, and South Dakota.

SUZANNE DUARTE is an online adjunct professor of deep ecology in the ecopsychology master's program at Naropa University. She has been an ecological writer, teacher, and activist for twenty years, and coauthored *Lessons of the Rainforest* (under the name Suzanne Head), published in 1990. She currently resides in Amsterdam, the Netherlands.

Considered the first truly professional writer to hail from Texas, **J. FRANK DOBIE**, teacher, storyteller, folklorist, historian, and author, was born September 26, 1888, on a ranch in the south Texas brush country of Live

Oak County. Raised in the toughening, physically bracing traditions of a remote ranching region, Dobie nonetheless developed an early love for language and literature. His mother encouraged reading, providing her children with mail-ordered books, and his father developed the boy's narrative sense with nightly readings of the King James version of the Bible. Following an unsuccessful ranching stint, Dobie wrote his wife, Bertha, that "in the university I am a wild man; in the wilds I am a scholar and a poet."

STEVE EDWARDS is a naturalist and educator living and teaching in the forests around Bend, Oregon. He has worked for the Oregon Musem of Science and Industry's Cascade Science School and The Nature Conservancy, and is presently an educator for Wolftree, Inc.

JOAN FOX's stories and poems have appeared in various journals; a novel excerpt was nominated for a Pushcart Prize. Where she lives with her family in the Southwest, a cougar stalking hikers deemed to be "not acting like a cougar" was exterminated.

GARY GILDNER was born in West Branch, Michigan. His twenty published books include *Blue Like the Heavens: New and Selected Poems*, *The Second Bridge* (a novel), *The Warsaw Sparks* and *My Grandfather's Book* (both memoirs), and *The Bunker in the Barley Fields*, which received the 1996 Iowa Poetry Prize. His new collection of short stories, *Somewhere Geese Are Flying*, was published by Michigan State University Press in 2004. He has also received a National Magazine Award for Fiction, Pushcart Prizes in fiction and nonfiction, the Robert Frost Fellowship, the William Carlos Williams and Theodore Roethke poetry prizes, and two National Endowment for the Arts fellowships. Gildner has been writer-in-residence at Reed College, Davidson College, Seattle University, and Michigan State University, and has been a Senior Fulbright Lecturer to Poland and to Czechoslovakia. He has given readings of his work at the Library of Congress, the Academy of American Poets, YM-YWHA in New York, the Manhattan Theatre Club, and at some 300 colleges and schools in the United States and abroad. Gary Gildner lives on a ranch in Idaho's Clearwater Mountains.

Perhaps the most recognizable face of the conservation movement, **JANE GOODALL** is the world's renowned primatologist-turned-activist who brought the lives of chimpanzees to the forefront of animal behavior studies with her groundbreaking research conducted in the field in Tanzania over four decades. A longtime champion of animals and their well-being,

Dr. Goodall, along with Genevieve, Princess di San Faustino, founded the Jane Goodall Institute in 1977. Today, her international environmental and humanitarian program for young people, Roots & Shoots, has 3,000 to 4,000 active groups in more than seventy countries. Dr. Jane Goodall is the author of many best-selling books, including her autobiography *A Reason for Hope* (Warner Books, 2000) and *Harvest for Hope: A Guide to Mindful Eating* (Warner Books, 2005).

WENDY KEEFOVER-RING is the director of the Carnivore Protection Program at Sinapu, an organization dedicated to improving the West for wild carnivores. Keefover-Ring received a Master of Arts degree in history from the University of Colorado at Boulder. She led a five-year campaign that helped reform how Colorado manages its puma population. She also watchdogs the federal predator-killing program, the USDA Wildlife Services. Her publications "Mountain Lions, Myths, and Media: A Critical Reevaluation of *Beast in the Garden*" and "Final Words About Beasts and Gardens" appeared in the December 2005 issue of *Environmental Law*. These essays debate radio reporter David Baron about the historical, scientific, and cultural understandings of pumas.

TED KERASOTE's writing has appeared in more than fifty periodicals, including *Audubon*, *National Geographic Traveler*, *Outside*, *Salon*, and the *New York Times*. His most recent books are *Out There: In the Wild in a Wired Age*, which won the National Outdoor Book Award, and the *New York Times* best seller *Merle's Door: Lessons from a Freethinking Dog*. He lives in Wyoming.

CHRISTINA KOHLRUSS lives, writes, and hikes in cougar territory in the foothills outside of Denver, where she occasionally glimpses a cougar that lives nearby. Like the last cougar she encountered, she is a mother — and her daughter will one day, hopefully, have her own cougar story to tell. She also enjoys practicing balancing energy and body work as a craniosacral therapist.

BARRY LOPEZ is a widely acclaimed author, notably of *Arctic Dreams* (Charles Scribner's Sons, 1986), for which he received the National Book Award; *Of Wolves and Men* (Scribner, 1979), a National Book Award finalist for which he received the John Burroughs and Christopher Medals; and eight works of fiction, including *Light Action in the Caribbean* and *Field Notes*. His essays are collected in two books, *Crossing Open Ground* and *About This*

Life. He contributes regularly to *Granta, The Georgia Review, Orion, Outside, The Paris Review, Manoa,* and other publications in the United States and abroad. In his nonfiction, Mr. Lopez writes often about the relationship between the physical landscape and human culture. In his fiction, he frequently addresses issues of intimacy, ethics, and identity. His work appears in dozens of anthologies, including *Best American Essays, Best Spiritual Writing,* and the "best" collections from *National Geographic, Outside, The Georgia Review, The Paris Review,* and other periodicals.

Mr. Lopez is a recipient of the Award in Literature from the American Academy of Arts and Letters; the John Hay Medal; Guggenheim, Lannan, and National Science Foundation fellowships; Pushcart Prizes in fiction and nonfiction; and other honors.

BK LOREN's work has garnered many literary awards, including the Mary Roberts Rinehart Nonfiction Fellowship, the Dana Award for the Novel, the D. H. Lawrence Fiction Award, and a Colorado Council for the Arts Fellowship. *The Way of the River* (repackaged and retitled *Tiger to the Bone*) was published by Lyons in 2001, and Loren's shorter works have been published in periodicals and anthologies, including *The Best American Spiritual Writing 2004, Women on the Verge, Two in the Wild, Orion, Parabola,* and *Utne.* She attended the University of Iowa Writers' Workshop and is currently completing a novel.

CARA BLESSLEY LOWE is a writer and photographer based in Jackson, Wyoming. In 2001, she cofounded The Cougar Fund. Cara's work has appeared in *The Gift of Rivers: True Stories of Life on the Water* (Traveler's Tales, 2000), *The Encyclopedia of Animal Behavior* (Greenwood Press, 2004), *Wyoming 24/7* (DK Books, 2004), and *The Natural World* (Mangelsen, 2007). Cara is the author of *Spirit of the Rockies: The Mountain Lions of Jackson Hole* and the editor of *Polar Dance: Born of the North Wind,* by Fred Bruemmer and Thomas D. Mangelsen (Images of Nature, 1997), which won the BEA Best of Small Press award in 1997.

STEVE PAVLIK teaches American Indian studies and native environmental science at Northwest Indian College, Bellingham, Washington. In all he has over thirty years of teaching experience in the field of American Indian education. He holds a master's degree in American Indian studies from the University of Arizona. His specialty areas include Native American religion and spirituality, traditional ecological knowledge, and ethnozoology. He has published extensively and is the coeditor (with Daniel R. Wildcat) of *Destroying Dogma: Vine Deloria Jr. and His Influence on American Society* (2006).

DAVID C. STONER has been involved with field studies of cougars since 1996. He received his BA from the University of California at Berkeley in 1992 and, following a long hiatus, went on to earn an MS from Utah State University. Stoner's research is focused on cougar population dynamics within the framework of landscape ecology and has been published in the *Journal of Wildlife Management*. He is currently working toward a PhD. Stoner lives in Logan with his wife, Lisa; their daughter, Hailey; and a cat named Indy.

LINDA SWEANOR is a cougar ecologist based in Colorado and coauthor of *Desert Puma: Evolutionary Ecology and Conservation of an Enduring Carnivore* (Island Press, 2001). Based on ten years of research conducted along with her husband, Ken Logan, the book is considered the seminal work on mountain lion biology.

PERMISSIONS AND SOURCES